# PEARL HARBOR

# HISTORY SMASHERS

*The* Mayflower

*Women's Right to Vote*

*Pearl Harbor*

# PEARL HARBOR

## KATE MESSNER

### ILLUSTRATED BY DYLAN MECONIS

*With special thanks to Maggie Tokuda-Hall, who served
as an early reader and consultant for this book*

RANDOM HOUSE 🏠 NEW YORK

Text copyright © 2021 by Kate Messner
Cover art and interior illustrations copyright © 2021 by Dylan Meconis

All rights reserved. Published in the United States by Random House Children's Books, a division of Penguin Random House LLC, New York.

Random House and the colophon are registered trademarks of Penguin Random House LLC.

Visit us on the Web! rhcbooks.com

Educators and librarians, for a variety of teaching tools, visit us at RHTeachersLibrarians.com

*Library of Congress Cataloging-in-Publication Data*
Names: Messner, Kate, author. | Meconis, Dylan, illustrator.
Title: Pearl Harbor / Kate Messner; illustrated by Dylan Meconis.
Description: First edition. | New York: Random House, [2021] | Series: History Smashers | Includes bibliographical references and index. | Audience: Ages 8–12.
Identifiers: LCCN 2019038351 | ISBN 978-0-593-12037-8 (trade) | ISBN 978-0-593-12038-5 (lib. bdg.) | ISBN 978-0-593-12039-2 (ebook)
Subjects: LCSH: Pearl Harbor (Hawaii), Attack on, 1941—Juvenile literature. | World War, 1939–1945—Causes—Juvenile literature. | United States—Foreign relations—Japan—Juvenile literature. | Japan—Foreign relations—United States—Juvenile literature.
Classification: LCC D767.92 .M47 2020 | DDC 940.54/26693—dc23

Printed in the United States of America
10 9 8 7 6 5 4 3 2 1
First Edition

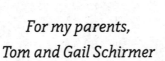

*For my parents,*
*Tom and Gail Schirmer*

# CONTENTS

You've probably heard the phrase "Remember Pearl Harbor." The Japanese attack on Pearl Harbor, Hawaii, is one of the most infamous events in American history. Maybe you've heard stories about that day—how the attack was a total surprise, with no warning whatsoever. How it lit up the morning sky on December 7, 1941, devastated the American fleet in the Pacific, and created immediate support for the United States to jump into World War II. But only parts of that story are true. When we look closely at documents from that time period, other parts come crashing down. Here's the real deal about the not-such-a-total-surprise attack that eventually led the United States into its second world war—along with some important but not-so-well-known stories about what happened next.

# ONE
## WAR
## OVERSEAS

People often tell the story of Pearl Harbor as if the Japanese attack in Hawaii happened completely out of the blue, with no warning and nothing to suggest there might be trouble. In reality, there were plenty of warning signs. But to understand how the attack on Pearl Harbor happened, we need to go back in time a bit.

Sometimes Americans think of 1941 as the beginning of World War II, but that was just when the United States got involved. The war had actually started two years earlier, in September 1939. That's when Nazi

Germany invaded Poland. France and Great Britain declared war on Germany two days later.

German troops march into Poland in September 1939.

It wasn't long before the war took over Europe. Between April and June 1940, Germany invaded Denmark, Norway, Luxembourg, the Netherlands, Belgium, and France. In June, Germany picked up some help from Italy, which declared war on Britain and France. And in July, Germany started bombing Great Britain.

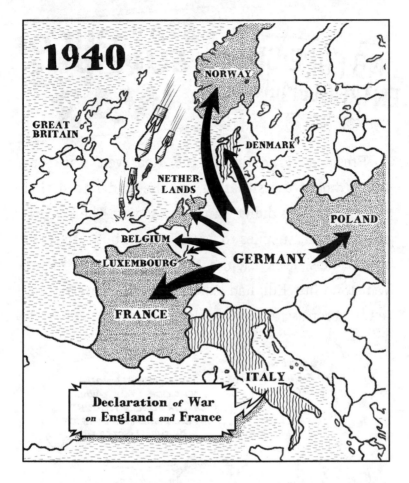

**1940**

GREAT BRITAIN

NORWAY

DENMARK

NETHER-LANDS

BELGIUM

LUXEMBOURG

POLAND

GERMANY

FRANCE

ITALY

Declaration *of* War *on* England *and* France

Sounds complicated, doesn't it? That's what most Americans thought, too, back when all this was happening. At the time, many people in the United States were in favor of a policy called isolationism, which basically means minding your own business.

## NO FOREIGN ENTANGLEMENTS

## STAY OUT OF EUROPE'S WAR

President Franklin Delano Roosevelt was concerned about the situation, but he understood that most Americans didn't want to go to war. The US government sent supplies to Great Britain but refused to send troops, even though Britain's prime minister, Winston Churchill, had asked for help. Roosevelt had made a promise to the American people.

WE WILL NOT PARTICIPATE IN FOREIGN WARS,

AND WE WILL NOT SEND OUR ARMY, NAVAL OR AIR FORCES TO FIGHT IN FOREIGN LANDS OUTSIDE OF THE AMERICAS,

EXCEPT IN CASE OF ATTACK.

But that promise got harder and harder to keep. Germany wasn't the only country trying to take over other nations. Japan was doing the same thing.

For two centuries, Japan had kept to itself, an isolated island nation. That started to change in 1853, when Commodore Matthew Perry led a US Navy expedition into what is now called Tokyo Bay, trying to open up Japan to trade with other nations.

By the 1920s, Japan was deeply involved in trade with other countries. It used some of the money that brought in to build a naval air force. Then Japan's military leaders decided it was time to expand the empire by taking more land.

In 1931, Japan invaded Manchuria, an area in northeast China. By 1937, it had launched a full-scale invasion of China. Hundreds of thousands of Chinese people were killed. The United States sent millions of dollars in relief funds to China but refused to get involved in the fighting.

When Germany started invading all those other countries in Europe, Japan's military leaders decided to grab even more territory. Since much of Europe was busy fighting the Nazis, it seemed like a perfect time for Japan to invade French Indochina, the part of East Asia that now includes Vietnam, Laos, and Cambodia. American leaders worried the Philippines, then under US control, might be next.

# COLONIALISM

Right about now, you might be thinking, "Hey, wait a minute! What are countries like France and the United States doing in East Asia anyway?" The answer to that question has to do with colonialism. That's the policy of taking over other countries, sending settlers, and using those countries' natural resources.

European nations, and later the United States, engaged in this practice throughout history. That's why many people of East Asia weren't in charge of their own lands back then. The United States had taken control of the Philippines from Spain in a war in 1898. And why did Spain have the Philippines to begin with? Because explorer Ferdinand Magellan had landed there in 1521 so Spain could take it from the people who lived there.

I CLAIM THESE ISLANDS FOR THE KING OF SPAIN!

Spain and other nations that engaged in colonialism often justified it by saying they were actually helping the people who lived there, by converting them to Christianity. It's probably no surprise to you that the people being invaded didn't appreciate that kind of "help." Interestingly enough, Japan also claimed it was "helping" when it launched its invasions in the 1930s—by freeing people from that old colonialism. But like the invaders who had come before, what the Japanese really wanted was natural resources.

With Japan showing no signs of stopping, President Roosevelt decided it was time for America to make a show of force. In 1940, he ordered America's Pacific Fleet, which had been stationed in San Diego, California, to Hawaii. The ships crossed the ocean and settled in at Pearl Harbor Naval Base on the island of Oahu. It was meant as a threat. Roosevelt thought moving the powerful fleet so close to Japan would show that the United States was ready to take action quickly if needed. Japan wouldn't want to tangle with America's powerful military, right?

But that plan didn't really work out. By September 1940, Japan was occupying northern French Indochina. Japan also signed a deal with Germany and Italy that month. The three nations called their agreement the Tripartite Pact. It promised that if any of those countries was attacked, the other two would defend it.

And that brings us to 1941, the year of the Pearl Harbor attack. The war in Europe was still going strong. In July, Japan sent troops into southern French Indochina.

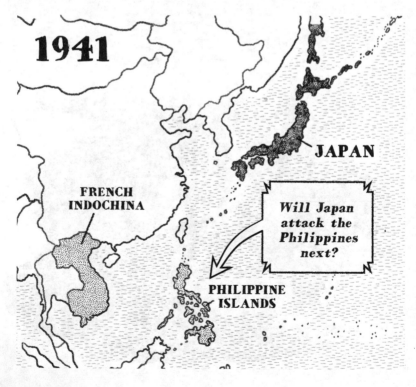

1941

JAPAN

FRENCH
INDOCHINA

Will Japan
attack the
Philippines
next?

PHILIPPINE
ISLANDS

Southern French Indochina was close to the Philippines, and US leaders worried that Japan might use its new position to stage an attack. Trying to prevent that, the United States cut off oil and iron exports to Japan. But that just created more tension. Most Americans still didn't want to get involved in any of this mess overseas, but it was looking more and more like the nation might be headed for war.

# THE HISTORY OF HAWAII

Pearl Harbor is remembered in history books as a terrible attack on American soil. But the truth is, in 1941, Hawaii hadn't been part of America for very long. It was just forty-three years earlier that the United States had taken the islands.

Hawaii's first settlers were Polynesian farmers and fishermen. Historians believe they crossed the ocean in canoes, arriving as early as 400 or 500 CE. For hundreds of years, they lived in small communities ruled by chieftains.

In 1778, English sea captain James Cook showed up on the island of Kauai. His arrival marked the beginning of change. With the help of western weapons and advice, one of the islands' chiefs, Kamehameha, was able to defeat other rulers, gain power, and unite the

islands under his rule. King Kamehameha is still honored as Hawaii's first king, with a celebration each June.

The first Christian missionaries arrived in the Hawaiian islands in 1820. These were white people who came from New England because they wanted to convert Hawaiian people to their religion.

Along with their Bibles, they brought diseases that wiped out most of Hawaii's Native population. When Cook first landed in the islands, at least 300,000, and perhaps more than half a million, Native Hawaiians lived there.

Less than a hundred years later, that number had dropped to 70,000 or less.

Meanwhile, white settlers interested in growing sugar bought lots and lots of land from Hawaiian people, who had little money. A group of white businessmen made a plan for America to take over the islands. In 1887, that group, the Hawaiian League, forced Hawaii's King Kalakaua to sign a new constitution at gunpoint. That document took away much of the king's power. It gave voting rights to foreign landowners and took rights away from thousands of people of Asian ancestry who'd lived in Hawaii for years.

A few years later, American colonists who controlled the islands' sugar industry overthrew the Native leader. The United States officially annexed, or took over, Hawaii in 1898.

## TWO
## WARNING
## SIGNS

"SURPRISE ATTACK . . ."
"OUT OF THE BLUE . . ."
"NO ONE COULD HAVE SEEN IT COMING . . ."

When people talk about Pearl Harbor, these phrases are often part of the story. But the truth is, while no one knew the exact date and time Japan would strike Hawaii, the attack wasn't a total surprise. Or at least it shouldn't have been. There were all kinds of warning signs. It didn't really come "out of the blue," and someone *did* see it coming, seventeen years before it happened.

In 1924, US Army officer William "Billy" Mitchell predicted the attack. Mitchell had coordinated a huge air campaign for the US Army during World War I. After that war, he argued that America needed a separate air force. (Back then, the army and navy had planes, but the US Air Force wouldn't exist as a separate branch of the military until 1947.)

Mitchell had been sent on a tour of the Pacific and Far East to evaluate the preparedness of US forces. When he got home, he warned that Japan's ideas about expanding its empire would eventually lead to war with the United States, starting with a surprise attack. And check out the details he included in his report. . . .

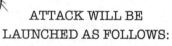

ATTACK WILL BE
LAUNCHED AS FOLLOWS:

BOMBARDMENT

ATTACK TO BE MADE ON
FORD'S [SIC] ISLAND
[IN PEARL HARBOR]
AT 7:30 A.M. . . .
ATTACK TO BE MADE
ON CLARK FIELD
[PHILIPPINES]
AT 10:40 A.M.

Mitchell nailed it, right down to the hour of the Pearl Harbor attack. The first bombs would be dropped just before 8:00 a.m. And Japan would, in fact, attack Clark Field in the Philippines a few hours later. But at the time of Mitchell's warning, nobody paid much attention. Perhaps that was because Mitchell had a reputation for being loud and opinionated. He had little patience for anyone who didn't agree with him, and he often criticized his bosses. Or maybe it was because people were busy and there was just too much to keep track of. Whatever the reason, they tossed Mitchell's report in a file and forgot about it.

Mitchell wasn't the only one who thought Pearl Harbor might be a target. In 1938, a US War Department survey said the same thing and added that if the Japanese did attack, there would be no warning. By early 1941, Japanese military leaders had their sights set on Pearl Harbor, too.

# 1941: WHO WAS IN CHARGE?

**THE PRESIDENT:** Franklin Delano Roosevelt had just been reelected president of the

United States. He knew that most of the American people didn't want war, so he kept talking with Japanese leaders, trying to come up with an agreement to keep the peace. But at the same time, Roosevelt believed that war might be inevitable.

**THE EMPEROR**: Hirohito was Japan's longest-ruling monarch. He served as emperor from 1926 to 1989. Officially, he was the country's leader in 1941, but historians believe that Japan's military leaders were holding most of the real power at that time.

**THE PRIME MINISTER**: Konoe Fumimaro was Japan's prime minister. He was trying to keep the military's power in check and hoped to avoid war with the United States. He spent months negotiating with America, but in October he was forced to resign over differences with Japan's army minister.

**ARCHITECT OF THE ATTACK**: Admiral Isoroku Yamamoto was in charge of the Japanese fleet and planned the attack on Pearl Harbor. Yamamoto had studied in America, at Harvard. He didn't want war with the United States, but he was convinced that if it happened, Japan's only chance would be to strike first. He'd called the US Pacific Fleet in Hawaii "a dagger being pointed at our

throat." In January 1941, he wrote to Japan's Navy Ministry, "The most important thing we have to do first . . . is to fiercely attack and destroy the US main fleet

21

at the outset of the war, so that the morale of the US Navy and the American people goes down to such an extent that it cannot be recovered."

**THE AVIATOR**: Commander Minoru Genda was a well-respected pilot who helped Yamamoto plan the Japanese attack on Pearl Harbor. Genda suggested that Japan strike Pearl Harbor in three waves, with bomber and fighter planes launched from aircraft carriers. Genda knew the attack had to be a surprise, so he urged Yamamoto to keep the plans top secret.

**THE NAVY MAN**: Frank Knox had been appointed US secretary of the navy in 1940. In January 1941, he wrote a letter to Secretary of War Henry Stimson, saying he believed a Japanese attack

was possible. Knox promised the military would take another look at whether Pearl Harbor was prepared.

## THE FLEET COMMANDER:

In February 1941, Admiral Husband E. Kimmel was appointed commander of the Pacific Fleet stationed at Pearl Harbor. Right away, he requested better defenses there. It was his job to train the fleet so it would be prepared for war.

## THE ARMY COMMANDER:

Lieutenant General Walter C. Short took command of the US Army's Hawaiian Department in February 1941. His main jobs at Pearl Harbor were to keep the fleet safe and to maintain the coastal defense of Oahu. Those jobs weren't easy; his equipment was old, and he didn't have enough men.

**THE AMBASSADOR**: Despite all the secrecy surrounding plans to attack Pearl Harbor, Joseph Grew, America's ambassador to Japan, caught wind of the plot within a month. He sent a cable  (a message transmitted via undersea cables) to Washington:

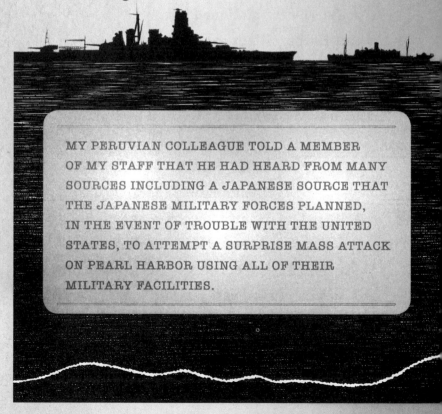

MY PERUVIAN COLLEAGUE TOLD A MEMBER
OF MY STAFF THAT HE HAD HEARD FROM MANY
SOURCES INCLUDING A JAPANESE SOURCE THAT
THE JAPANESE MILITARY FORCES PLANNED,
IN THE EVENT OF TROUBLE WITH THE UNITED
STATES, TO ATTEMPT A SURPRISE MASS ATTACK
ON PEARL HARBOR USING ALL OF THEIR
MILITARY FACILITIES.

There it was—a warning of what was about to happen, clear as day. So why wasn't America ready? The truth is, no one took Grew's warning very seriously. Military officials had decided that Japan was probably going to attack the Philippines instead.

By February 1941, Yamamoto was fine-tuning his idea to attack Pearl Harbor. The plan was to destroy the American battleships and aircraft carriers stationed there. Yamamoto figured that would give Japan six months to conquer more of Asia before the United States could rebuild its fleet.

## LIKE SOMETHING OUT OF A NOVEL

A 1925 novel called *The Great Pacific War* by Hector C. Bywater included a Japanese attack on American naval forces in the Pacific. Could Yamamoto have gotten the idea for his attack on Pearl Harbor from this book? No one knows

for sure, but the book was translated into Japanese, and there are some reports that Yamamoto had read it. Either way, an attack on Pearl Harbor made sense to Japanese military leaders at the time.

Japan wanted to build its empire so it could have more natural resources like iron, oil, rubber, and tin. It wanted to expand farther, into Malaya, the Philippines, and the Dutch East Indies, and hoped that an early attack on Pearl Harbor would keep America from getting in the way.

American military leaders had obviously thought about the possibility of an attack. In March, commanders of the army and navy air fleets in Hawaii wrote a memo outlining a plan to defend Oahu. It suggested that the military start regular air patrols around the island, going as far out to sea as possible so they'd be more likely to spot signs of a coming attack. That was a great idea, but with a shortage of both people and planes, it was easier said than done.

Meanwhile, back in Japan, Commander Minoru Genda was put in charge of preparing the men who would carry out the attack. His pilots trained through the summer at Kagoshima Bay in southern Japan, which had a layout similar to Pearl Harbor. That was important when it came to torpedoes, the underwater

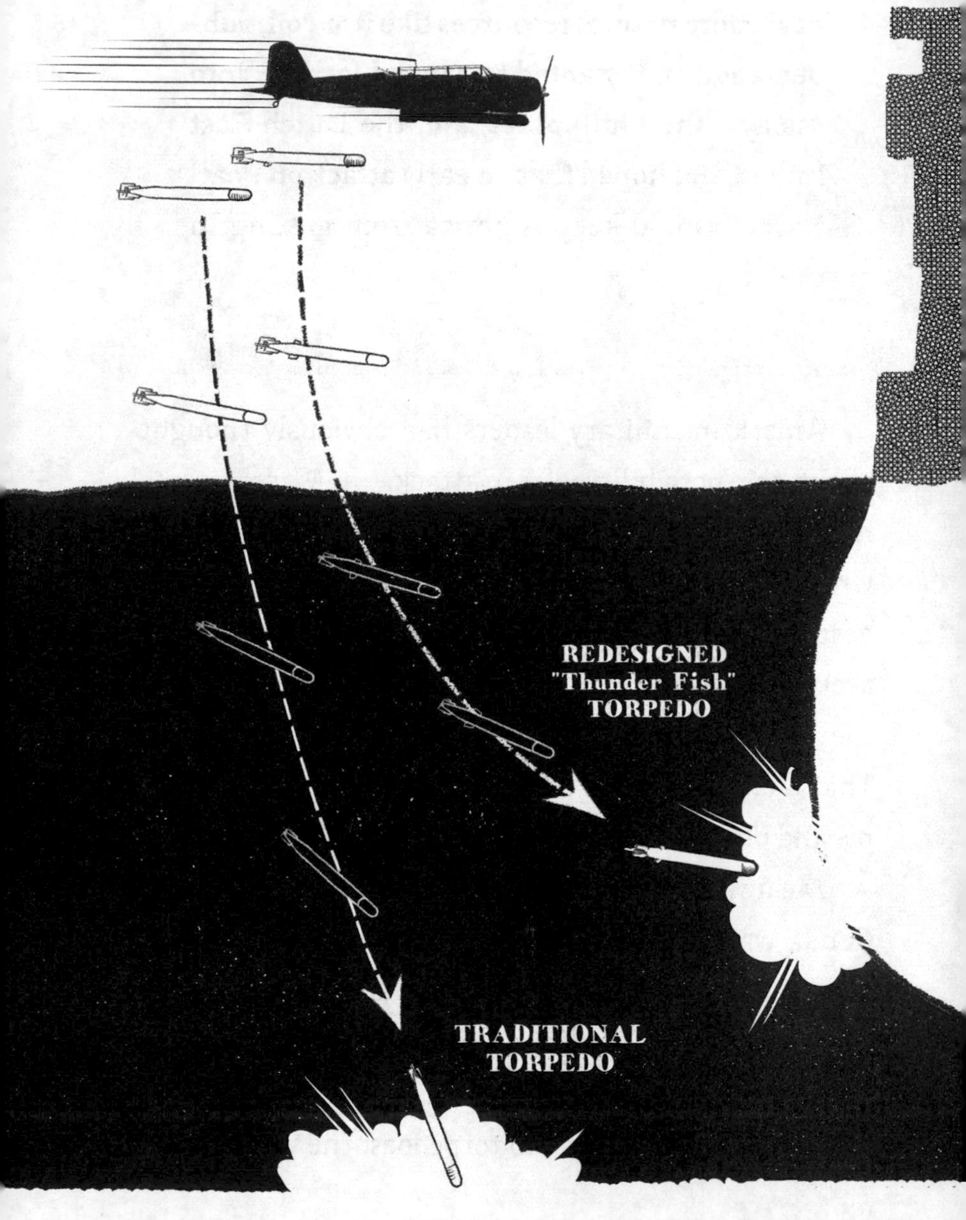

REDESIGNED
"Thunder Fish"
TORPEDO

TRADITIONAL
TORPEDO

missiles that explode when they hit a target. Most torpedoes had to be dropped into water that was at least sixty to seventy feet deep or they'd hit bottom before they reached their target. But Pearl Harbor was only thirty to thirty-five feet deep, so the Japanese had to redesign their torpedoes. They came up with a new version, known as the Thunder Fish, that worked in shallower water.

This torpedo was discovered during a dredging operation in Pearl Harbor in 1991. The torpedo was nearly intact when it came up from the sea in the bucket of a crane. Its warhead was still armed, so navy explosives experts took it out to sea and detonated it. After the blast, they were able to recover this section of the rear part of the torpedo, which is now on display at the Pearl Harbor Visitor Center.

You might think that with all this training going on in Japan, America would at least hear rumors about what was happening. But Yamamoto and the other military leaders were careful to keep the plan a secret. They were *so* careful that Japan's ambassador to the United States, Kichisaburō Nomura, claimed that even he didn't know about it.

The United States had intelligence officers and code breakers working to figure out what Japan might be planning. In the summer of 1940, they'd cracked the code that was used to send messages to Japanese diplomats. That was thanks to a new code-breaking tool called "Purple." It was a special machine that helped code breakers decrypt information. They called that decoded intelligence "Magic." But they hadn't managed to crack the code that Japan's military used, so they weren't getting all the information that was being relayed. By late 1941, American intelligence officials had intercepted enough messages to know that war was imminent. They understood that Japan was planning some kind of attack. They just didn't know precisely when or where it was going to happen.

Intelligence gathering was tricky business. Sometimes there simply weren't any messages to decode.

Many messages that were decoded also had to be translated. And sometimes, when code breakers did manage to learn important information, it wasn't communicated to the right people.

In September 1941, American intelligence officers found out that Japan's navy was looking for information about where Pearl Harbor's battleships were located. You'd think that would be a huge warning sign, but it was mostly ignored. Nobody even told Admiral Kimmel that Japan was asking where he kept his ships.

In the fall of 1941, Japan sent special envoy Saburo

Kurusu to Washington, DC, to help Nomura in talks with US officials. Japan was in a tough spot. The iron and oil embargo that the United States had started after the Japanese invasion of French Indochina prevented Japan from getting the natural resources it needed. Emperor Hirohito was hoping for an agreement to keep the peace, but by then Japan had a new prime minister, the more warlike Hideki Tojo. He didn't think Japan should give in to any of the US demands.

Still, Japan's ambassador presented a proposal: if the United States would start trading with Japan again, the Japanese agreed not to make any new

advances into East Asia. The two sides kept meeting and talking that fall. But at the same time, Japan was getting ready to attack. Negotiations were still happening when the Japanese fleet set out for Hawaii in late November. Six aircraft carriers braved enormous waves in the middle of the night, keeping radio silence so they wouldn't be detected.

On November 27, 1941, US Secretary of State Cordell Hull rejected Japan's offer. A promise of no more invasions wasn't enough. The United States demanded that Japan pull out of China completely . . . or else. Japan considered that a declaration of war.

"IF JAPAN AND THE UNITED STATES REACHED SOME KIND OF AGREEMENT AND SUCCEEDED IN THE PEACE NEGOTIATIONS, WE WOULD RETURN TO JAPAN. BUT I HAD NO IDEA ABOUT THAT. I COULD ONLY PRAY TO GOD."

—JAPANESE TORPEDO PLANE PILOT LT. HIRATA MATSUMURA

Two days later, Hull got his hands on a copy of a speech that Tojo had given to inspire Japan's military. It sounded like the sort of speech someone would give when they were getting ready to go to war. Hull called Roosevelt, who was on a short vacation in Georgia. Hull told the president a Japanese attack seemed imminent and suggested that he come home. So Roosevelt packed his bags and headed back to Washington the next morning.

On December 1, Emperor Hirohito met with Prime Minister Tojo and gave the go-ahead for war. Chuichi Nagumo, the Japanese admiral who would oversee the attack on Pearl Harbor, was on his way there when he got a message from Yamamoto.

"Climb Mount Niitaka 1208"

THIS WAS THE SIGNAL TO GO AHEAD WITH THE ATTACK.

THE NUMBERS 1208 REFERRED TO THE DATE FOR THE ATTACK.

You might be thinking, "Hey, wait! The strike on Pearl Harbor happened on December 7, didn't it?" You're right about that. But Japan is on the other side of the international date line, so the morning of December 7 in Hawaii was actually December 8 in Japan.

As the Japanese fleet made its way to Pearl Harbor, the United States had some chances to learn what was happening. On November 27, Kimmel and Short had received a "war warning" from DC, letting them know that Japan might be preparing to hit an American military target in the Pacific. So on December 2, Kimmel asked for an update on Japan's aircraft carriers. He was told that some of them were missing. Just . . . missing. *Maybe* they were somewhere in Japan's home waters, but nobody was sure.

You might think that would be a major red flag and that it would prompt Kimmel to increase those patrols around Oahu. But that's not what happened. At the time, both Kimmel and Short were more worried that Japanese Americans who lived in Oahu might sabotage America's military.

In December 1941, more than a third of the people in Hawaii were of Japanese descent. Many were

American citizens who'd lived on Oahu their whole lives. There had been absolutely no intelligence to suggest they were planning anything to harm their country. But military leaders still thought that was a major concern. Their fear was based on prejudice—not actual information—and it distracted them from the real threat. It even led them to line up the planes at Hickam Field, an army air base on Oahu, so they'd be safer from sabotage—a decision that we now know made the planes a better target for the air attack that was coming.

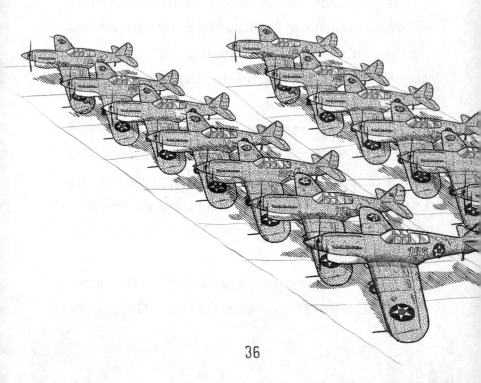

On December 3, American intelligence officers intercepted and decoded even more Japanese messages. One asked for additional reports about the location of the warships at Pearl Harbor. There was also a conversation between the Japanese ambassadors to the United States and Prime Minister Tojo. The ambassadors were wondering if it might still be possible to avoid war if they met with the Americans once more. Tojo replied that it would be inappropriate for them to suggest another meeting at that point.

Meanwhile, those "missing" Japanese aircraft carriers were getting closer and closer to Pearl Harbor.

# THREE
## COUNTDOWN TO DISASTER

By December 6, 1941, the Japanese fleet was approaching Hawaii. Still, no one had spotted it. Everything was on schedule for the planned attack the next day. Japan had spies in Honolulu who had been following the movement of the American ships. They thought all the big ships would be at Pearl Harbor that morning. Since December 7 was a Sunday, some of the military men would be sleeping late—all the better for the surprise attack.

On the way to Pearl Harbor, Japanese pilots studied maps. They took quizzes on what different kinds of ships looked like from the air. They were ready. America was not.

ON OAHU, DECEMBER 6, 1941, FELT LIKE AN ORDINARY SATURDAY.

THE UNIVERSITY OF HAWAII FOOTBALL TEAM PLAYED AGAINST WILLAMETTE UNIVERSITY AND WON, 20–6.

SAILORS WHO HAD THE DAY OFF WENT INTO HONOLULU AND BOUGHT CHRISTMAS CARDS TO SEND HOME TO THEIR FAMILIES.

SOME OF THE OFFICERS PLAYED GOLF AT FORT SHAFTER.

MEANWHILE, THE BATTLESHIPS WERE LINED UP AT PEARL HARBOR.

BUT THE AIRCRAFT CARRIERS WERE OUT AT SEA.

THOUSANDS OF MILES AWAY, IN AMERICA'S CAPITAL . . .

. . . THE PRESIDENT WAS STILL HOPING TO AVOID A WAR.

Tokyo had sent a fourteen-page memo to its embassy in the United States that day. A note told Japan's ambassador not to deliver the memo to US officials until half an hour before the attack on Pearl Harbor. In 1907, Japan had signed an international treaty promising not to launch a war without "previous and explicit warning." So Japan *did* give the United States a warning—just not a very long one. Half an hour wasn't enough time for people in Washington to do anything at all about the attack.

But American intelligence officers intercepted that memo early. Most of it, anyway. They got all but the last page. Those first thirteen pages explained why Japan was still upset about America's embargo and unhappy with the talks so far.

When President Roosevelt read the memo, he said, "This means war." But he made one last attempt to keep the peace, by sending Emperor Hirohito a letter. It began with the long history of friendship between Japan and the United States. Roosevelt made it clear that Japan should withdraw its troops from Indochina and stop pushing into other nations. He wrapped up with a plea for peace.

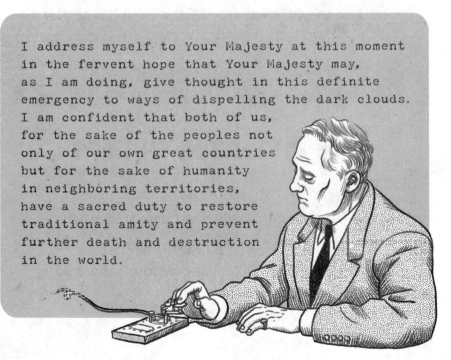

I address myself to Your Majesty at this moment in the fervent hope that Your Majesty may, as I am doing, give thought in this definite emergency to ways of dispelling the dark clouds. I am confident that both of us, for the sake of the peoples not only of our own great countries but for the sake of humanity in neighboring territories, have a sacred duty to restore traditional amity and prevent further death and destruction in the world.

Might the last-minute letter make a difference? The truth is, it never had a chance, because the note didn't make it to Hirohito on time. It was sent via telegram to the ambassador, with directions to deliver it to the emperor as soon as possible. But somewhere along the way, the letter got delayed. By the time it finally reached Hirohito, the attack was almost underway.

The men at Pearl Harbor didn't know any of this. So the night before the attack, many of them were out listening to music. There was a Battle of Music that night at Bloch Arena—a competition between the bands on the different ships. Each band had to play a swing number, a ballad, and one specialty tune. They all played a song for the jitterbug contest, too.

## THE JITTERBUG CHAMPS

Ten-year-old Patricia "Patsy" Campbell was at the Battle of Music with her dad, a navy officer. She'd been tapping her feet all night until finally her dad asked one of the sailors to dance with her.

That sailor was seventeen-year-old Jack Evans, and he was happy to have a partner for the jitterbug contest. All the girls he'd asked to dance that night had turned him down. When the contest started, the two danced up a storm. Patsy was so light that Jack could toss her right up in the air as they danced, no problem. The judges loved them!

After three rounds, Patsy and Jack were announced as the jitterbug champs! The judges gave them each a trophy. Patricia's is now on display in the Pearl Harbor Visitor Center.

The magic of the jitterbug contest didn't last, though. Bombs fell on Pearl Harbor the very next morning. Patsy didn't even know if the kind boy who'd danced with her had survived. But decades later, they'd meet again. They danced together one more time in 2001, on the sixtieth anniversary of Pearl Harbor.

At 6:00 a.m. on December 7, the Japanese fleet was in position, 220 miles north of Oahu. The ships had traveled for ten days, undetected. Now hundreds of Japanese pilots gathered on the decks of their aircraft carriers to get their instructions. They boarded their planes, fastened their helmets, and started their engines. The propellers began to spin, and soon 183 planes would take off from the decks, all headed for Pearl Harbor.

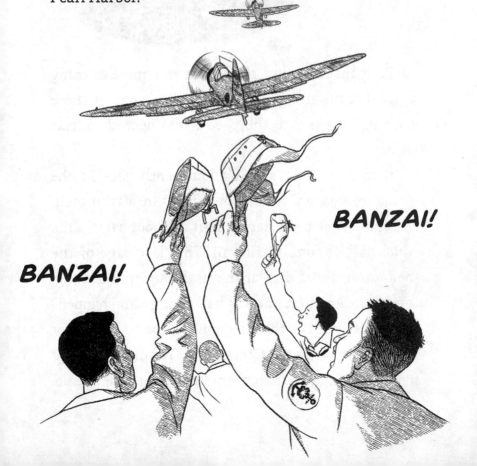

JAPANESE COMMANDER AND BOMBER PILOT MITSUO FUCHIDA LED THE FIRST WAVE OF AIR ATTACKS ON PEARL HARBOR.

Early that morning, there were even more warning signs that an attack was coming. But none of those warnings made it to the people who needed to hear them.

Remember that missing fourteenth page of the memo from Japan? American officials in Washington, DC, finally got their hands on it at about 11:00 a.m., which is 5:00 a.m. in Hawaii. That last page of the memo announced that Japan was through negotiating. It made it clear that war was happening—and happening *very* soon. Still, there were no clues about when or where it would begin. Officials in Washington sent a message to Hawaii to let them know about the memo.

But that message wasn't marked urgent, so it didn't get delivered in time.

The first real sign of trouble in Hawaii happened when a sailor spotted the periscope of a submarine sticking out of the waves early that morning.

There weren't supposed to be any American subs in the harbor at that time, so he reported it. That report might have served as an early warning, but you can probably guess by now what happened. That information never made it to the right people, either.

A little later that morning, just after 6:30, the small two-man Japanese submarine was spotted again. This time, Seaman First Class Alan Sanford and other sailors on the USS *Ward* saw it trying to sneak into the harbor. Sanford shared the story in an oral history interview in 1991.

IT LOOKED LIKE A FIFTY-GALLON OIL DRUM ON TOP OF MAYBE THREE OR FOUR OF 'EM THAT WERE LAID DOWN BELOW IT, WITH A BROOMSTICK STICKING UP. AND OF COURSE, THAT BROOMSTICK WAS THE PERISCOPE.

THE MEN KNEW WHAT THEY HAD TO DO, BUT IT WAS A JOB, HANDLING AMMUNITION IN THE ROUGH SEAS.

"AND HERE YOU ARE, STAGGERING ALL OVER THAT ROLLING, PITCHING DECK WITH LIVE AMMUNITION . . ."

"WE FIRED AND YOU COULD WATCH DOWN THE END OF THE BARREL, AND YOU COULD SEE THAT THE PROJECTILE JUST BARELY MISSED THE SUB."

"I THOUGHT IF IT HAD ANOTHER COAT OF PAINT ON THE SUB, IT MIGHT HAVE ACTIVATED THE GRAZE FUSE. THAT'S HOW CLOSE I THINK WE CAME."

BUT THEN ANOTHER GUN FIRED. . . .

THIS TIME, THEY HIT THE JAPANESE SUB, KILLING THE TWO MEN INSIDE.

49

America's military didn't realize it at the time, but that little submarine was part of Japan's carefully planned attack. In fact, about thirty submarines had made the secret trip to Pearl Harbor along with the aircraft carriers. The plan was for them to surround Oahu and attack any American ships that tried to escape from the harbor once the raid was underway. Five of those subs had midget subs, and it was one of those two-man subs that the USS *Ward* shot at that morning.

You might think this would be the big warning sign. A Japanese submarine taken out in the harbor, in the middle of an American military base! The men from the USS *Ward* radioed headquarters to report what had happened, but no one was too concerned. It seemed like an isolated incident. No big deal.

When the Japanese bombers were just 137 miles out, less than an hour from Oahu, America had one more chance to discover their plan and sound the warning. Believe it or not, US military actually *saw* those incoming Japanese planes on radar. The technology was pretty new at the time. It allowed the military to use radio waves to "see" what was in the sky for miles around. And just before 7:00 a.m., the two men on duty saw something unusual.

# HOW RADAR WORKS

Radar equipment transmits radio waves, which bounce off solid objects they encounter.

When that signal bounces back, it's captured by a receiver. That return signal shows up as a blip on the radar, and it can tell the person watching the screen how big the object is, and how far away.

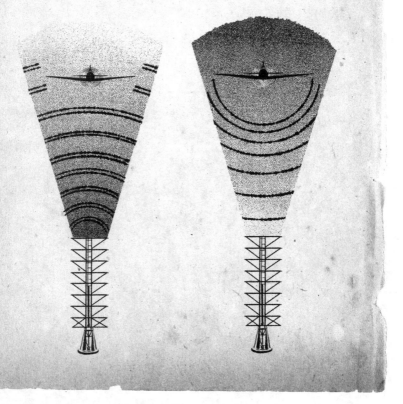

Privates Joseph Lockard and George Elliot were still learning how to use the radar. Lockard was showing Elliot how the whole system worked when they picked up a blip on the screen—incoming planes at a time when no flights were supposed to be arriving. At first, the two privates thought it was a mistake. They weren't sure if the equipment was malfunctioning, or if they were even using it right. But a few minutes later, at 7:02 a.m., they picked up the signal again. This time, it was 132 miles out.

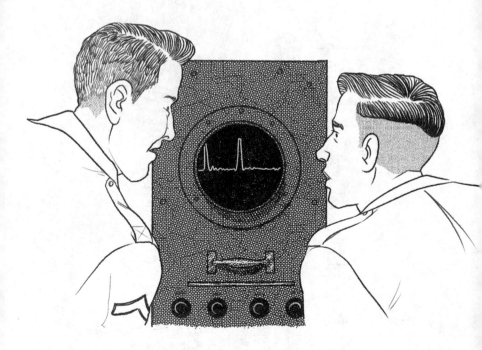

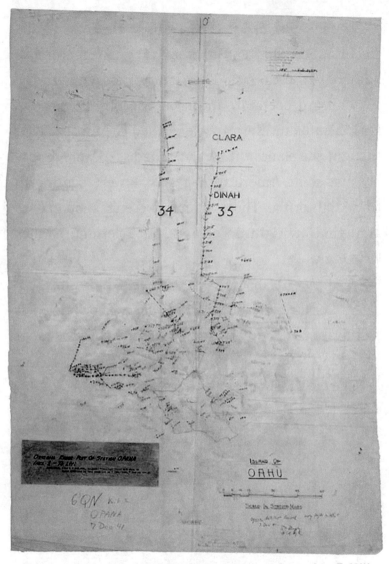

This original radar plot from the morning of December 7, 1941,
is now on display at the Pearl Harbor Visitor Center.

The men decided to report this to the information center at Fort Shafter. But when they called, everyone had gone to breakfast. They left a message with the switchboard operator, and soon the officer on duty, First Lieutenant Kermit Tyler, called them back. Tyler thought the planes the two men had seen were probably just some American B-17s that were coming in from California. Those planes weren't supposed to arrive in Hawaii until 8:00 a.m., but Tyler figured they were early.

"Don't worry about it," he told the two privates.

So Lockard and Elliot didn't worry about it. Their shift was over. They left, and nobody checked the radar again.

They really should have worried about it.

# FOUR
# THIS IS NOT A DRILL!

On the morning of December 7, more than 185 American ships and service boats were moored at Pearl Harbor—everything from destroyers, minesweepers, and battleships to tugboats and barges. But the aircraft carriers—among Japan's most important targets—weren't there. They'd been sent to deliver planes to the Philippines and hadn't returned yet.

The battleships were all lined up, though. On board, sailors were finishing breakfast and writing Christmas cards. You might guess that with everything that had been happening, they'd be worried that a Japanese attack could come any day. But most weren't. At least not the younger men. As far as they knew, Japan and America were still negotiating to avoid war. Many still figured they'd work things out. They had no idea that enemy planes were already closing in on Pearl Harbor.

It was 7:49 a.m. when Japanese Commander Mitsuo Fuchida saw Pearl Harbor from the air and gave the order to attack.

"*Tora*" is the Japanese word for "tiger." That message meant the planes had managed to approach undetected. The attack was underway!

Torpedo planes dove into position. Bombers peeled off to hit nearby airfields so the American planes wouldn't be available to fight back.

# THE PILOT IN PAJAMAS

Four American planes were able to take off from the army's Wheeler Field while the attack was underway. A pilot named Philip Rasmussen flew one of them. Rasmussen had just woken up when the bombing began. He rushed to the flight line in his pajamas but found that nearly all the planes were destroyed or on fire. The only aircraft that seemed to be okay were a few outdated P-36 Hawks. Still sporting his pj's, Rasmussen jumped into one of those and took off with Japanese planes shooting at him.

Rasmussen was in a firefight with eleven Japanese planes at Kaneohe Bay. He shot down one of them, but when enemy fire hit his plane, he had to go back. When Rasmussen landed his damaged plane, it was riddled with more than five hundred bullet holes. He earned a Silver Star for his actions that morning.

It was 7:55 a.m. when Lieutenant Commander Logan Ramsey saw a low-flying plane approaching Ford Island. At first, he thought it was an American pilot, but then he saw the plane drop a bomb and realized Hawaii was under attack. That's when the first alarm went out via telegram:

**AIR RAID ON
PEARL HARBOR X
THIS IS NO DRILL**

Remember those planes that had been lined up so nicely to keep them safe from sabotage? They were easy targets.

But within minutes, American servicemen began to fight back.

Sailors fired machine guns and antiaircraft munitions at the Japanese planes. By the end of the morning, US forces would bring down twenty-nine enemy planes. But some of that antiaircraft ammunition fell on neighborhoods around Honolulu, killing civilians and damaging homes and schools.

News of the attack spread quickly in the areas close to Pearl Harbor. James Lee, who volunteers at Pearl Harbor National Memorial now, was eleven years old when the attack happened.

Lee tells Pearl Harbor visitors how he heard the roar of diving planes early that morning and ran to the railroad tracks so he could sit and watch. Like many others, he thought it was just American planes practicing in case of an attack. It was fun and exciting until he realized what he was actually seeing. Smoke and fire filled the harbor. Lee saw little boats going around, trying to rescue men from the water.

Just before the attack, USS *Arizona* sailors had been preparing for the morning flag-raising ceremony. The band was on deck with their instruments, ready to play "The Star-Spangled Banner," when the men saw a group of planes approaching. At first they thought it was a drill. But then the explosions rang out—and sailors noticed that these planes had red circles on their wings. It was the Japanese symbol of the rising sun. That's when the American sailors realized this was no drill.

# PEARL HARBOR UNDER ATTACK!

CLARK SIMMONS, A MESS ATTENDANT WHO SERVED FOOD ON THE USS *UTAH*, WAS STILL BELOWDECKS WHEN A FELLOW SAILOR TOLD HIM ABOUT THE ATTACK.

THE SHIP IN FRONT OF US JUST BLEW UP!

HE WAS TALKING ABOUT THE RALEIGH,

ONE OF THE FIRST JAPANESE TARGETS THAT MORNING.

SIMMONS RAN TO LOOK OUT THE PORTHOLE.

HE WAS JUST IN TIME TO SEE A JAPANESE PLANE FLY IN TO DROP A TORPEDO.

IT WAS HEADED STRAIGHT FOR THE UTAH!

SIMMONS FELT THE WHOLE SHIP SHAKE WHEN THE TORPEDO BLASTED INTO THE HULL.

WHEN A SECOND TORPEDO HIT, THE SHIP BEGAN TO LIST TO ONE SIDE.

IT WAS TIME TO ABANDON SHIP.

SIMMONS AND OTHER SAILORS LEAPED—

AND STARTED SWIMMING.

JAPANESE PLANES FILLED THE SKY, SHOOTING DOWN AT THEM.

EVENTUALLY SIMMONS MADE IT TO FORD ISLAND. HE'D BEEN INJURED BUT WOULD SURVIVE THE ATTACK.

BUT THE USS UTAH WAS ANOTHER STORY.

IT WOULD NEVER FLOAT AGAIN.

# A SEGREGATED NAVY

In 1941, America's military was segregated. That meant that Simmons and other African American men weren't allowed to serve in the same units, or even visit the ship's store at the same time, as sailors who were white. Only certain jobs were available to Black men. They could do support work like cook or serve in mess halls, or handle ammunition, but they weren't allowed in combat roles. In spite of this racism in the military, many African American men acted heroically throughout World War II.

As word spread about the attack, Japanese Americans on Oahu felt a sense of panic.

Harriet Kuwamoto, whose parents were from Japan, was a nurse who spent December 7 helping out at the health department. Years later, she told an oral history interviewer about the fear her family felt that day, the worry that somehow, as people of Japanese descent, they might be blamed. Her brother even burned the beautiful Japanese scroll her family had hanging on the wall of their home.

Meanwhile, the attack on Pearl Harbor's battleships came fast and fierce. Gene Huggins, a carpenter's mate on the USS *Vestal* repair ship, saw the torpedo planes swooping in that morning.

"THEY'D COME LOW, DROP THE TORPEDO, AND YOU COULD FOLLOW THAT TORPEDO RIGHT UNTIL IT HIT THE *OKLAHOMA* AND *WEST VIRGINIA* TIED UP RIGHT IN FRONT OF US THERE. AND THEN THE PLANES WOULD BANK, AND THEY WOULD COME RIGHT OVER US. . . . YOU COULD HAVE HIT THEM WITH A SLINGSHOT. . . . YOU COULD SEE THE PILOT WITH HIS GOGGLES AND EVERYTHING." —GENE HUGGINS, USS *VESTAL*

The USS *Oklahoma* was an early target.

A. H. MORTENSEN WAS A SAILOR ON THE USS OKLAHOMA. HE WOKE UP TO THE AIR RAID WARNING THAT MORNING.

THIS IS NOT A DRILL!

WITHIN MINUTES, THE FIRST TORPEDO HIT.

BOOM!

IT LIFTED THE SHIP RIGHT OUT OF THE WATER.

WHEN THE SECOND AND THIRD TORPEDOES BLASTED INTO THE SHIP, MORTENSEN HIT THE DECK. THERE WERE EVEN MORE TO COME. "IT JUST SEEMED TO BE A SWARM. IT WAS JUST ONE AFTER THE OTHER."

RIGHT AWAY, THE SHIP STARTED TO LIST. IT WAS GOING TO CAPSIZE!

THE COMPARTMENT MORTENSEN WAS IN BEGAN TO FILL WITH WATER.

HE AND SOME FELLOW SAILORS TREADED WATER AS THE SHIP ROTATED

THEY WERE RUNNING OUT OF TIME.

THEIR ONLY HOPE WAS THE PORTHOLE, NOW UNDERWATER. SO MORTENSEN TOOK A DEEP BREATH AND DOVE. . . .

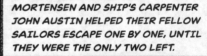

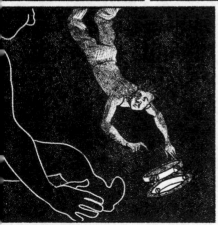

MORTENSEN AND SHIP'S CARPENTER JOHN AUSTIN HELPED THEIR FELLOW SAILORS ESCAPE ONE BY ONE, UNTIL THEY WERE THE ONLY TWO LEFT.

69

AUSTIN WAS TOO BIG TO FIT THROUGH THE TINY OPENING. HE REACHED OVER AND HELD THE PORT OPEN FOR MORTENSEN.

MORTENSEN CLIMBED THROUGH . . .

. . . AND SWAM FOR THE SURFACE.

A THICK COAT OF OIL COVERED THE SEA. HE DOG-PADDLED THROUGH IT TOWARD HIS OVERTURNED SHIP.

WITH SHRAPNEL FALLING ALL AROUND, THE MEN WERE FINALLY RESCUED BY A MOTOR LAUNCH.

THEY WERE THE LUCKY ONES —429 OF THEIR FELLOW CREWMEN ON THE USS OKLAHOMA DIED IN THE ATTACK . . .

. . . INCLUDING NAVY CHIEF WARRANT OFFICER JOHN ARNOLD AUSTIN, WHO HELPED HIS FELLOW SAILORS ESCAPE BUT NEVER MADE IT OFF THE SHIP HIMSELF. AFTER HIS DEATH, HE WAS AWARDED THE NAVY CROSS FOR VALOR IN COMBAT.

Within eleven minutes of being hit, the USS *Oklahoma* capsized. Sailors climbed onto the hull to search for survivors. They knew some men couldn't get out—they could hear tapping from inside. Rescuers cut through the hull and were able to save another thirty-two men. But many were still trapped. One sailor said the tapping went on for two days before it finally stopped.

Within minutes that morning, torpedoes also sank the *West Virginia*. They blew holes in the *Nevada*, the *Utah*, the *California*, and the *Maryland*. But the greatest loss of life would be on the USS *Arizona*.

The huge battleship had first launched from New York City in 1914. The USS *Arizona* was modernized after World War I so it could fire at greater range. With 50-caliber machine guns on both masts, the ship became a symbol of American strength. But the morning of December 7 would change everything.

# A PEARL HARBOR HERO

Dorie Miller enlisted in the navy in 1939. Because he was Black, he was allowed to serve only as a mess attendant. Miller was stationed at Pearl Harbor on the USS *West Virginia*. He was gathering laundry when the Japanese attack began. Miller rushed to his battle station, but by the time he got there, the ship had already been hit by a torpedo. Miller carried wounded men to safety, and when he found an unmanned antiaircraft gun, he started firing at the enemy, even though he'd never been trained to use it.

The story of Dorie Miller is one that's taken on legendary status because his heroism helped inspire people to fight for civil rights in America. In an interview after the Pearl Harbor attack, Miller said he thought he hit one of the Japanese planes. Some versions of the story have him bringing down as many as six planes, but nobody's sure of the number.

Dorie Miller was awarded the Navy Cross for his valor at Pearl Harbor, the first African American to be honored with that distinction.

# FIVE
# THE USS
# *ARIZONA*

We hear a lot about the torpedoes that came barreling underwater at America's battleships at Pearl Harbor, but they weren't responsible for the greatest loss of life. That morning, Japanese planes were also dropping bombs that could pierce armor. Eight of them hit the USS *Arizona*.

The first bomb blasted through the deck near the rear of the ship and started a fire. A second bomb hit near the antiaircraft deck, closer to the front of the ship. A third one hit the port, or left, side of the great battleship. Two more bombs hit that repair ship, the USS *Vestal,* which was tied up to the *Arizona*.

USS *Arizona* survivor Jim Miller was in one of the ship's turrets when the early bombs hit. "There was a tremendous shaking," he said. He wasn't hurt, though, so he stepped out of the turret to see what was happening. "The forward part of the ship . . . was just solid flame." He saw burned and bleeding men on the deck and decided that his first priority was to help fight the fire. Other men joined in, too.

"It looked like a blow torch coming out of the hole, where the bomb went in," said USS *Arizona* survivor Glenn Lane. He grabbed a hose and tried to help, but there was no water pressure. "So we got just a few drops coming out of that stupid hose."

The flames were already out of control. Sailors did the best they could to help their injured friends on deck and rescue those who were trapped in the smoke and fumes in compartments below. All the while, Japanese gunners were shooting at them from above.

# The Bombing of the USS *Arizona*

THE NEXT BOMB, A 1,760-POUND (800 KG) ARMOR-PIERCING SHELL, DROPPED FROM A HIGH-ALTITUDE JAPANESE PLANE—WOULD BE DEVASTATING.

IT BLASTED THROUGH THE USS ARIZONA'S FORWARD MAGAZINE, WHERE THE GUNPOWDER WAS KEPT.

SOME ESCAPED BY CROSSING HAND OVER HAND ON A LINE TOSSED OVER FROM THE *VESTAL*.

IT WAS A TREACHEROUS ESCAPE— SWINGING ABOVE THE WATER WITH PATCHES OF OIL BURNING BELOW.

C'MON, ONE MORE SWING! YOU CAN MAKE IT!

MEANWHILE, GLENN LANE FOUGHT HIS WAY TO THE SURFACE OF THE OIL-COVERED SEA.

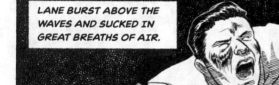

LANE BURST ABOVE THE WAVES AND SUCKED IN GREAT BREATHS OF AIR.

"I LOOKED BACK. . . . I COULDN'T SEE A LIVING PERSON ON THE SHIP. NOT ONE."

SO LANE STARTED SWIMMING FOR THE USS *NEVADA*. ALL AROUND HIM, MEN STRUGGLED TO SURVIVE.

FINALLY, COVERED IN SLICK BLACK OIL, LANE CLIMBED UP THE GANGWAY. HE'D MADE IT!

BUT THE TROUBLE WASN'T OVER YET. . . .

At about 8:45 that morning, there was a lull in the noise and chaos. The Japanese planes seemed to be gone. But what Lane and the other men didn't realize was that a second wave of planes was already on the way. More Japanese high-level bombers, fighters, and dive bombers swarmed over Oahu just before 9:00 a.m. They attacked the airfields, hit the battleship *Pennsylvania*, blew up oil tanks, and blasted the bow off the destroyer *Shaw*.

Explosion of the USS *Shaw* during the attack on Pearl Harbor

The USS *Nevada* had been torpedoed in the first wave of the attack. It was damaged and taking on water but managed to get its engines started. Sailors around the harbor watched as the great ship headed for the open sea. But the slow-moving battleship was a perfect target for that second wave of Japanese planes. If it sank in the channel, it could block other American ships from leaving.

That's when poor Glenn Lane, who'd survived one bombing, found himself under attack again. He was already burned from the fires on the *Arizona*, but he helped man a gun on the *Nevada* as the Japanese planes flew over. They hit the *Nevada* hard, with bombs that knocked Lane and the other sailors from their feet. When the planes finally flew off, the ship was in flames. This time, Lane found himself fighting the fire with wet mattresses.

"WE THREW A MATTRESS IN THE WATER, [WOULD] SOAK IT, AND THEN THROW IT UP TO YOU AND YOU PUT IT ON YOUR BACK AND YOU GO UP THE LADDER . . . ON THE BOAT DECK, WHERE THE FIRES WERE. YOU THROW THAT MATTRESS DOWN THERE AND STOMP ON IT, AND THEN RUN BACK AND GET ANOTHER MATTRESS."

Lane kept fighting the fires and trying to save injured shipmates until finally his injuries overcame him and he collapsed. The *Nevada* had to give in, too. It was taking on more and more water. Rather than let it sink where it could cut off the narrow channel, the *Nevada*'s crew ran it aground.

Meanwhile, rescuers took Glenn Lane to the hospital ship in a small motor launch. On the way, he felt the impact of what had just happened:

"I WOULD GO DOWN ALL ALONG THE BATTLESHIPS — HERE'S THE CALIFORNIA SINKING AND HERE'S THE OKLAHOMA, CAPSIZED. HERE'S THE WEST VIRGINIA, BURNED AND SINKING, SUNK. AND BEHIND HER, THE ARIZONA IS IN A SHAMBLES. I SAID, 'GOOD GOD, THERE'S OUR BATTLE FLEET.'"

The attack had lasted only two hours, but it was intense. By the time it ended, Japanese bombers and torpedoes had sunk or damaged eight American battleships, along with at least ten other vessels. A total of 347 American planes were destroyed or damaged. And the loss of life was devastating. More than 2,400 Americans were killed in the attack, and over a thousand more wounded. On the USS *Arizona* alone, 1,177 men were killed.

# BROTHERS AND SHIPMATES

In December 1941, thirty-seven sets of brothers were serving on the USS *Arizona*. Most of these were two brothers serving together, but three families—the Beckers, Dohertys, and Murdocks—had three brothers on the ship. Only one brother from each set survived.

Of the seventy-nine brothers on the *Arizona*, sixty-three died, including twenty-three full sets of brothers. The only pair of brothers who survived were Kenneth and Russell Warriner. A father and son, Thomas Augusta Free and William Thomas Free, also served together on the *Arizona*. Neither survived the attack.

Because of the awful losses so many families suffered at Pearl Harbor, military officials tried to discourage family members from 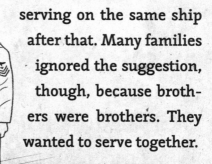 serving on the same ship after that. Many families ignored the suggestion, though, because brothers were brothers. They wanted to serve together.

Not all of the Pearl Harbor casualties were servicemen. Sixty-eight civilians died as well. Antiaircraft ammunition fell around the city of Honolulu, damaging buildings and setting homes on fire.

By 10:00 a.m., the Japanese planes were flying back to their aircraft carrier in the Pacific. Originally, the attack on Pearl Harbor had been planned in three waves. There had only been two, but officers decided it had been successful. Only twenty-nine Japanese planes were lost, and the damage to the American fleet was huge. There would be no third wave. Instead, the Japanese force started for home. Meanwhile, America was left to treat the wounded, recover the dead, and make plans for war.

## DID ALL OF JAPAN SUPPORT THE ATTACK?

You might think that in order to pull off an attack like this, the entire nation of Japan would have had to support it. But that wasn't really the case. In fact, even the plan's architect had some real doubts about whether it was a good idea. Yamamoto worried that attacking Pearl Harbor would make the United States angry. He feared it would launch a war that Japan couldn't win. He ended up being right.

## SIX
# AFTER THE ATTACK

When the attack on Pearl Harbor ended, the sky was black with smoke. The *Arizona* was engulfed in flames and would keep burning for two and a half days. All around the battleships, sailors walked the landings, searching for missing brothers and friends, while rescuers worked to save as many as possible.

Minutes after the attack began, the hospital ship USS *Solace* had begun sending out motor launches to rescue the wounded. When we hear about heroes from Pearl Harbor, the stories are often about men. But the truth is, without the women who cared for the wounded that day, there would have been far fewer survivors.

At first, USS *Solace* chief nurse Grace Lally was in shock as she watched the *Arizona* burn. But she snapped out of it and got to work, preparing an emergency ward for the patients she knew would be on the way. Lally led a crew of a dozen nurses on the hospital ship. They started treating the wounded by 8:20 that morning and continued for two months, until the last of the patients could be moved to land-based hospitals. Nurses on board the USS *Solace* treated nearly three hundred wounded sailors on December 7.

One of those nurses, Ann Danyo Willgrube, had joined the Navy Nurse Corps in 1940. She served as an operating room nurse on the *Solace*. In 1981, she wrote a letter about her experience to a high school student who was working on a report.

Dear Tommy:
While talking to your mother today, I learned that you are interested in learning more about that Day of Infamy—December 7, 1941. . . .

WILLGRUBE WROTE HOW EXCITED SHE'D BEEN TO BE STATIONED IN HAWAII AS A YOUNG NURSE.

SHE ESPECIALLY LOVED WAIKIKI BEACH.

It was only a city block long, and always crowded because the fleet was there.

BUT THEN CAME THE MORNING OF DECEMBER 7.

The ship shook and everyone ran out on deck to see what happened. I looked out the porthole in my room and saw smoke pouring out of the _Arizona_.

The next minute, our chief nurse burst into the room and told me to dress quickly and report to the quarter-deck for duty.

Casualties were coming aboard very fast and sent to the various wards as soon as their injuries were evaluated.

I was then assigned to the operating room because that was my specialty and help was needed there....

That day, December 7th, everyone stayed on duty around the clock until all casualties were taken care of.

I have never ceased being amazed at how quickly we reacted to the surprise attack on Pearl Harbor.... We never had disaster drills, yet when we realized that we were actually at war, every person on board that ship seemed to know instinctively what to do.

I hope you enjoy a happy holiday season.

Sincerely,

Ann D. Willgrube

The hospital ship wasn't the only place wounded sailors ended up. All around Oahu, nurses worked around the clock saving lives. The number of wounded men was overwhelming. Nurses sometimes marked patients' foreheads with lipstick as part of triage, a process for sorting victims based on how serious their injuries are. They knew they couldn't save everyone. But they kept working even as bombs exploded around them.

Annie Fox, the head nurse at Hickam Field, spent the hours after the attack administering anesthesia and treating wounds. She earned a medal for her heroic work after the attack.

Myrtle Watson was the only nurse in her ward at Schofield Hospital when the attack began. She'd arrived early for her weekend shift and was bringing patients out to the veranda when the Japanese planes arrived. As bullets flew and plaster fell around her, Watson hurried to get everyone back inside. She piled mattresses around patients to protect them as the base was being attacked. Then she stayed on duty for three days straight to help those who'd been wounded.

Civilians came together to pitch in after the attack, too. Residents of Honolulu showed up to donate blood. An elementary school was converted to a makeshift hospital. Women who worked on Honolulu's Hotel Street gave up their rooms for wounded soldiers and helped with first aid.

# WOMEN AT WAR

Treating the wounded after the Pearl Harbor attack was just the beginning of women's service during World War II. Soon, they'd step up for all kinds of noncombat roles. Many took over farms and factory jobs when the men went off to fight. The army created a unit called WARD, the Women's Air Raid Defense, whose members replaced the men from the Army Signal Corps when they were needed in combat.

Women of WARD

WARD was made up of civilian women who were trained to read radar as part of the army's new Aircraft Warning Service. They used movable, colored arrows to plot radar readings on a big map. They kept track of the flights around Hawaii so any enemy planes could be quickly spotted and identified. Later in the war, women around the country served in other groups to do all kinds of non-combat jobs.

Members of the ANC, or Army Nurse Corps, worked as nurses in field hospitals around the world. They treated wounded

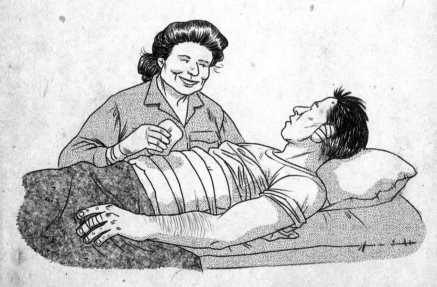

soldiers on the ground as well as in planes and trains when they had to be transported to a bigger hospital.

WASPs, or members of the Women Airforce Service Pilots, were the first women to fly US military aircraft. They tested planes for manufacturers while male pilots were away at war. They also flew planes that needed to be moved from one place to another and delivered supplies.

WAVES, Women Accepted for Volunteer Emergency Service, helped to support the navy, mostly serving as nurses or doing paperwork. But many of the women who'd studied science in college were involved in forecasting weather and doing research for the military.

Members of WAAC, the Women's Army Auxiliary Corps, were enlisted to do basic jobs like typing at first. But many ended up being trained to be mechanics, pilots, or code breakers. In 1943, Congress passed

a law to drop "Auxiliary" from the group's name and make it part of the US Army so women who served would receive the same benefits as men.

A recruitment poster for WAAC

Even after the attack was over, people in Hawaii worried there might be more planes on the way. Rumors swirled around the island. There were false reports of Japanese troops landing on Oahu. Hawaii's director of civil defense ordered nighttime blackouts. Families had to stay in their homes with no lights on at all. The darkness would make it harder for enemy planes to target areas where people lived. Oahu resident Enid Slinzak remembered putting denim over the windows to block out the light.

"IF THEY SAW ANYONE THAT HAD A LIGHT ON, THEY'D SHOOT IT OUT OR SHOOT ANYONE. . . . YOU WEREN'T ALLOWED OUT ON THE STREET AFTER TEN O'CLOCK AT NIGHT."

It was an especially scary time for families of Japanese descent. Almost immediately after the attack, soldiers showed up at many of their homes to question them.

THEY LOADED HARRY GODA INTO THE TRUCK AND DROVE TO A PRISON ACROSS TOWN. THERE WERE OTHER MEN THERE, TOO.

THEN THE QUESTIONING BEGAN. FROM SOLDIERS AND CIVILIANS.

ARE YOU A CITIZEN OF THE UNITED STATES?

YES.

WHAT WERE YOU DOING DECEMBER 7?

TEACHING JAPANESE TO SMALL CHILDREN AFTER GRAMMAR SCHOOL.

WHY WERE YOU TEACHING JAPANESE?

IT WAS JUST MY WORK.

YOU [ARE] NOT SUPPOSED TO TEACH JAPANESE TO THE PEOPLE OF THE UNITED STATES!

THEN ONE OF THE MEN SAID SOMETHING GODA WOULD NEVER, EVER FORGET.

YOU'RE NOT A CITIZEN, ALTHOUGH YOU WERE BORN IN HAWAII.

THEN THE MAN CALLED HIM A RACIAL SLUR. HARRY GODA DIDN'T SAY ANYTHING ELSE AFTER THAT.

While all this was happening on Oahu, officials in Washington were scrambling to respond. President Roosevelt was notified of the Pearl Harbor attack not long after it began. That night, he briefed his cabinet.

The next day, America would be at war.

# SEVEN

# THIS IS WAR!

D ecember 7, 1941, marked a turning point in World War II. When war first broke out in Europe, most Americans wanted to stay out of it. But President Roosevelt knew that an attack on US soil changed everything. On December 8, 1941, he gave a now-famous speech to Congress and the nation.

YESTERDAY, DECEMBER 7, 1941— A DATE WHICH WILL LIVE IN INFAMY—THE UNITED STATES OF AMERICA WAS SUDDENLY AND DELIBERATELY ATTACKED BY NAVAL AND AIR FORCES OF THE EMPIRE OF JAPAN.

THE UNITED STATES WAS AT PEACE WITH THAT NATION AND, AT THE SOLICITATION OF JAPAN,

WAS STILL IN CONVERSATION WITH ITS GOVERNMENT AND ITS EMPEROR LOOKING TOWARD THE MAINTENANCE OF PEACE IN THE PACIFIC.

INDEED, ONE HOUR AFTER JAPANESE AIR SQUADRONS HAD COMMENCED BOMBING IN THE AMERICAN ISLAND OF OAHU,

THE JAPANESE AMBASSADOR TO THE UNITED STATES AND HIS COLLEAGUE DELIVERED TO OUR SECRETARY OF STATE A FORMAL REPLY TO A RECENT AMERICAN MESSAGE.

AND WHILE THIS REPLY STATED THAT IT SEEMED USELESS TO CONTINUE THE EXISTING DIPLOMATIC NEGOTIATIONS,

IT CONTAINED NO THREAT OR HINT OF WAR OR ARMED ATTACK.

IT WILL BE RECORDED THAT THE DISTANCE OF HAWAII FROM JAPAN MAKES IT OBVIOUS THAT THE ATTACK WAS DELIBERATELY PLANNED MANY DAYS OR EVEN WEEKS AGO.

DURING THE INTERVENING TIME THE JAPANESE GOVERNMENT HAS DELIBERATELY SOUGHT TO DECEIVE THE UNITED STATES BY FALSE STATEMENTS AND EXPRESSIONS OF HOPE FOR CONTINUED PEACE.

THE ATTACK YESTERDAY ON THE HAWAIIAN ISLANDS HAS CAUSED SEVERE DAMAGE TO AMERICAN NAVAL AND MILITARY FORCES.

I REGRET TO TELL YOU THAT VERY MANY AMERICAN LIVES HAVE BEEN LOST.

ROOSEVELT TOLD THE NATION HOW JAPAN HAD ALSO ATTACKED MALAYA, HONG KONG, GUAM,

JAPAN

MIDWAY

HONG KONG

PHILIPPINES

WAKE ISLAND

PEARL HARBOR

GUAM

MALAYA

THE PHILIPPINES, WAKE ISLAND, AND MIDWAY ISLAND.

AS COMMANDER IN CHIEF OF THE ARMY AND NAVY I HAVE DIRECTED THAT ALL MEASURES BE TAKEN FOR OUR DEFENSE.

BUT ALWAYS WILL OUR WHOLE NATION REMEMBER THE CHARACTER OF THE ONSLAUGHT AGAINST US.

WITH CONFIDENCE IN OUR ARMED FORCES— WITH THE UNBOUNDING DETERMINATION OF OUR PEOPLE—

WE WILL GAIN THE INEVITABLE TRIUMPH— SO HELP US GOD.

I ASK THAT THE CONGRESS DECLARE THAT SINCE THE UNPROVOKED AND DASTARDLY ATTACK BY JAPAN ON SUNDAY, DECEMBER 7, 1941,

A STATE OF WAR HAS EXISTED BETWEEN THE UNITED STATES AND THE JAPANESE EMPIRE.

THEN HE ASKED CONGRESS TO DECLARE WAR.

Roosevelt's address has come to be known as the "Day of Infamy" speech. The word "infamy" means the same thing as the word "fame"—but in a bad way. Something that's infamous is famous, but not for good reasons. And here's something most people don't know—the president's first draft didn't even have that word in it!

DRAFT No. 1                                          December 7, 1941.

### PROPOSED MESSAGE TO THE CONGRESS

Yesterday, December 7, 1941, a date which will live in ~~world history~~ *infamy*

the United States of America was ~~simultaneously~~ *suddenly* and deliberately attacked

by naval and air forces of the Empire of Japan ~~without warning~~.

The United States was at the moment at peace with that nation and was

~~still in~~ ~~continuing the~~ conversations with its Government and its Emperor looking

toward the maintenance of peace in the Pacific.  Indeed, one hour after

Japanese air squadrons had commenced bombing in ~~Hawaii and the Philippines~~ *Oahu*

the Japanese Ambassador to the United States and his colleague delivered

to the Secretary of State a formal reply to a ~~former~~ *recent American* message ~~from the~~

~~Secretary.~~ *While* This reply ~~contained a statement~~ *stated* that diplomatic negotiations *it seemed useless to continue*

~~must be considered at an end, but~~ *it* contained no threat ~~and no~~ hint of ~~an~~ *or war or*

armed attack.

It will be recorded that the distance ~~of Hawaii, and especially~~ of

Hawaii from Japan make*s* it obvious that the ~~y~~ attack ~~were~~ *was* deliberately

planned many days *or years* ago.  During the intervening time the Japanese Govern-

ment has deliberately sought to deceive the United States by false

statements and expressions of hope for continued peace.

106

Roosevelt's draft of the talk, which is on file at the National Archives, shows a bunch of handwritten changes. That famous first line originally called December 7 "a date which will live in world history" instead of "a date which will live in infamy." Looking at Roosevelt's revisions to the talk, it's clear that he thought about every word. He knew the speech was an important one, and it did its job. People who had been against the war came around to support America's involvement.

But America declared war on only Japan that day. That was because of another revision. America's war secretary had originally drafted a declaration of war against Japan, Germany, *and* Italy, dated December 8. But Roosevelt asked for a declaration only against Japan.

It didn't matter much in the end. Remember that Tripartite Pact that Japan had signed with Germany and Italy? It promised that if any of those countries were attacked, the other two would defend it. So on December 11, Italy and Germany declared war on the United States. Then Roosevelt gave a speech to Congress, asking for a declaration of war on all three nations.

# WHO WAS TO BLAME?

America was devastated by the attack on Pearl Harbor. In the days and months that followed, everyone wanted to know how such a surprise attack could have happened. Some people blamed Navy Admiral Husband Kimmel and Army Lieutenant General Walter Short for missing the warning signs. Others pointed to Roosevelt. Some even claimed that he knew about the attack but let it happen because he wanted America to join the war. There's no direct evidence to support that theory.

It is true that there were warning signs that an attack from Japan might be coming, though. An Office of Naval Intelligence memo sent on December 4, 1941, reported that Japan was collecting information as it prepared for a possible conflict with the United States. It said Japan was "paying particular attention to the West Coast, the Panama Canal and the Territory of Hawaii." But many American officials still thought that first strike was likely to happen in the Philippines. No one had detected the Japanese fleet that was already heading for Hawaii.

After Pearl Harbor, there were lots of meetings about who was to blame—a board of inquiry and military tribunals and even a congressional investigation. Ultimately, neither Kimmel nor Short were convicted of the military crime called dereliction of duty, which basically means slacking off and not doing your job. But both had already lost their commands and were forced to retire from the military in disgrace. They were blamed for not doing more to prevent the attack.

The men's supporters argued that they were being treated unfairly and should have their good reputations back. The controversy raged on for years. Finally, in 1999, long after both men had died, the US Senate voted to exonerate them, which means to clear them of any wrongdoing.

After the attack on Pearl Harbor, one of the first orders of business was seeing if any of the damaged ships could be saved.

Recovery work began immediately. The navy and civilian teams worked together to raise the sunken ships, fix them up, and get them back into service.

At times, it felt like an impossible mission. The *Nevada* had been hit by bombs and blasted with a torpedo near the bow. The *California* had been ravaged by torpedoes, and was on fire before it sank into the mud near its moorings.

Divers plunged into the muddy waters of Pearl Harbor and searched the ships for blast holes. Other workers designed great big patches to cover the holes. Then teams of recovery workers used those patches, along with pumps, cables, winches, and big, air-filled pontoons called cofferdams to bring the ships back to the surface.

Bombs and torpedoes had sunk the *West Virginia* as well.

"Inside, the *West Virginia* looked as if she had been crumpled like paper in a giant hand," wrote *New York Times* reporter Robert Trumbull, a year after the attack. When engineers managed to raise the ship, they had to rebuild a lot of it. "The compartments belowdecks were half-filled with rubble—rotting stuff that exuded an overpowering stench." Trumbull wrote that the men worked tirelessly and "treated the maimed battleship as a mother would tend to a sick child."

Divers spent day after day in the water, trying to raise and save the ships. Their work was difficult and dangerous. They had to deal with ammunition left on the ships.

> One day an unexploded 1,750-pound bomb was discovered, held in a section of steel that it had penetrated. An officer risked his life to unscrew the live fuses.
>
> —ROBERT TRUMBULL, *NEW YORK TIMES* REPORTER

But the saddest, most difficult work was recovering the remains of men who died in the attack. Some of the dead were laid to rest in local cemeteries. Others were buried in temporary graves until the war ended and their families could bring them home to the mainland for burial. Some were buried at the National Memorial Cemetery of the Pacific, or the Punchbowl, which was built in 1948. The cemetery site is an extinct volcano called Punchbowl Crater. Others who died at Pearl Harbor never left their ships. The *Utah* and the *Arizona* are the final resting place for hundreds of American servicemen killed in the attack.

All but three of the vessels damaged or sunk at Pearl Harbor would rise and return to battle. The USS *Arizona* would never float again. The *Utah* and the *Oklahoma* were also damaged beyond repair. But some, including the battleship *Pennsylvania,* were only lightly damaged and returned to service right away. Others required more work.

The USS *Nevada,* which had run aground during the second wave of the attack, got some temporary repairs and then sailed to Puget Sound in Washington for more repairs and new guns.

The ship was back in service in less than a year. Others were repaired and sent back out between 1942 and 1944.

Japan had hoped that attacking Pearl Harbor would cripple the Pacific Fleet and destroy American morale. But in fact, the opposite happened. It's true that the attack damaged the fleet, but it also made the United States determined to fight back. All of Yamamoto's concerns about the attack were coming true.

# DID HE REALLY SAY THAT?

A 1970 movie called *Tora! Tora! Tora!* shows the Japanese admiral Isoroku Yamamoto reflecting on whether the attack on Pearl Harbor was effective.

I FEAR ALL WE HAVE DONE IS TO AWAKEN A SLEEPING GIANT AND FILL HIM WITH A TERRIBLE RESOLVE.

That movie is so popular that it's taken on a life of its own—and that famous "sleeping giant" quote is often attributed to the *real* Yamamoto. It's true that the man who planned the Pearl Harbor attack wasn't 100 percent convinced it was the best idea. But there's absolutely no evidence that he said those words.

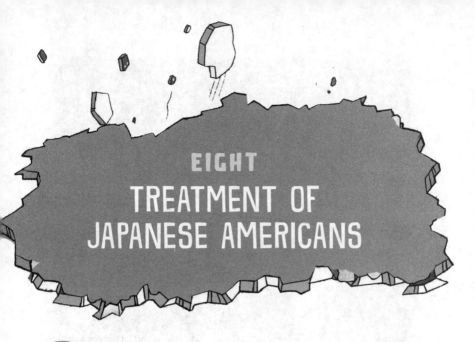

# EIGHT
# TREATMENT OF JAPANESE AMERICANS

Sometimes a disaster brings out the best in people. Sometimes it brings out the worst. The attack on Pearl Harbor did both.

There's no question that the bombing of Pearl Harbor brought people together. In the hours and days that followed the attack, Americans pitched in to help one another in so many ways. Boy Scouts and Girl Scouts volunteered to answer phones, deliver bandages, and black out windows in government buildings. Citizens of Hawaii donated blood. They volunteered to help the wounded and do pretty much any other job that needed to be done. And when the president declared war, men

San Francisco, December 1941: Men stand in line to enlist
in the military after the attack on Pearl Harbor.

and women from all over America stepped forward to
join the effort however they could.

But not everyone's help was welcome. Even as patriotism brought people together, fear, ignorance, and
racism drove them apart.

Americans of Japanese descent ended up being
blamed for the attack even though they had absolutely
nothing to do with it. You might be wondering how
that could happen when there was no evidence at all.

But it was—and still is—common for entire groups of people to be unfairly blamed when something goes wrong. This is especially true of immigrants, people of color, and those who are part of religious minorities. Even today, anti-immigrant talk is a big part of some candidates' campaigns for public office.

And remember, there was a lot of finger-pointing after the Pearl Harbor attack. People wanted to know how such a terrible thing could have happened on American soil. They wanted someone to blame. And it's easier to blame someone who doesn't look like you.

Some people pointed fingers at Kimmel and Short or at Secretary of the Navy Frank Knox. Knox wasn't happy about that, so he did what he could to shift the blame. He insisted, without evidence, that Japanese people in America had somehow helped with the attack. Knox went so far as to call for the internment—or imprisonment—of Japanese people, even if they were American citizens. His accusations added fuel to the already widespread prejudice against Japanese Americans. Newspaper headlines fed the fear.

One newspaper writer used a racial slur and compared people of Japanese descent to venomous snakes. He said it didn't matter that many were American citizens.

THIS WORD WAS A RACIAL SLUR FOR JAPANESE PEOPLE. EVEN SOME NEWSPAPERS USED IT, FUELING PREJUDICE.

SUBS RAID CALIFORNIA SHIPS

NEW WEST COAST RAIDS FEARED

ARMY ORDE SABOTAGE ALERT HER

# The Question of Japanese-Americans
## BY W. H. ANDERSON

"A viper is nonetheless a viper wherever the egg is hatched."

With all of this happening, you might think white people would stick up for their neighbors of Japanese ancestry, but few did. Most white people in America were caught up in the fear and hate. Many Japanese immigrants and their children had become successful farmers and business owners. Some people were jealous of them, and many were simply racist. They fought to have Japanese American people removed from their communities. And the US government listened.

About two months after the attack, President Roosevelt signed an executive order that resulted in many thousands of men, women, and children of Japanese ancestry being rounded up, forced from their homes, and imprisoned.

FEBRUARY 19, 1942
EXECUTIVE ORDER,

AUTHORIZING THE
SECRETARY OF WAR,
TO PRESCRIBE
MILITARY AREAS

The executive order said that the United States needed to take precautions against spying and sabotage. It authorized the secretary of war and military commanders to set up "military areas" from which people could be suddenly excluded, even if they'd lived there for years. Those military areas were pretty much the entire West Coast of the United States. They included California, Oregon, and Washington, where many families of Japanese descent had homes, farms, and businesses. Now those families would be forced out and imprisoned. The government also set up "internment camps," where people who were removed from military areas would be held.

## HIDING THE TRUTH

Really, these "internment camps" were prison camps. But the government called them internment camps because it sounded nicer. When we use gentler language to make something bad sound better, that's called a euphemism. Some euphemisms are harmless, like saying that someone "passed away" instead of that they died. But in cases like this, using a euphemism hides the truth about what really happened—the fact that thousands of American citizens of Japanese descent were ripped from their homes, rounded up in fairground horse stables, and then moved to prison camps.

Roosevelt's executive order gave a huge amount of power to the government. Normally, in order to be thrown in jail in America, a person has to be formally accused of a crime, with the promise of a fair trial to come. But this order bypassed those rights. It gave officials permission to throw people in prison camps and to keep them there for as long as they felt like it. Even though the document never mentioned Japanese people, everybody knew that's who Roosevelt was talking about. As a result of that executive order, more than 120,000 men, women, and children of Japanese ancestry were forced from their homes and sent to these prison camps. Two-thirds of those people were American citizens, but that didn't matter to the government.

ONCE THE ORDER WAS ISSUED, PEOPLE OF JAPANESE ANCESTRY WERE FORCED TO LEAVE THEIR HOMES.

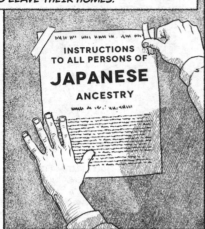

MANY HAD TO SELL THEIR HOUSES, BELONGINGS, AND BUSINESSES, OFTEN AT A HUGE LOSS.

THEY COULD BRING ONLY WHAT THEY COULD CARRY.

FIRST, THEY WERE TRANSPORTED AS PRISONERS, SURROUNDED BY MILITARY GUARDS, TO TEMPORARY DETENTION CENTERS.

THE CENTERS WERE SET UP AT FAIRGROUNDS AND RACETRACKS. PEOPLE HAD TO SLEEP IN STABLES OR LIVESTOCK STALLS, OR SOMETIMES WITHOUT SHELTER AT ALL.

EVENTUALLY, THEY WERE MOVED TO THE PRISON CAMPS, ALL LOCATED IN REMOTE AREAS.

IN 1943, THE US WAR DEPARTMENT MADE A FILM TO JUSTIFY THIS IMPRISONMENT OF JAPANESE AMERICANS.

JAPANESE RELOCATION

WE KNEW THAT SOME AMONG THEM WERE POTENTIALLY DANGEROUS.

MOST WERE LOYAL, BUT NO ONE KNEW WHAT WOULD HAPPEN AMONG THIS CONCENTRATED POPULATION IF JAPANESE FORCES SHOULD TRY TO INVADE OUR SHORES.

THE VIDEO PLAYS UPBEAT MUSIC AS JAPANESE PEOPLE GET OFF BUSES AT A CAMP. THEY DON'T LOOK HAPPY.

"NATURALLY, THE NEWCOMERS LOOKED ABOUT WITH SOME CURIOSITY. THEY WERE IN A NEW AREA, ON LAND THAT WAS RAW, UNTAMED, BUT FULL OF OPPORTUNITY. HERE THEY WOULD BUILD SCHOOLS, EDUCATE THEIR CHILDREN, RECLAIM THE DESERT."

BUT THE VIDEO DOES ITS BEST TO MAKE THEIR FORCED RELOCATION SOUND LIKE AN OPPORTUNITY.

"SPECIAL EMPHASIS WAS PUT ON THE HEALTH AND CARE OF THESE AMERICAN CHILDREN OF JAPANESE DESCENT."

BUT THAT TIDY VERSION OF HISTORY CAME CRASHING DOWN WHEN PEOPLE SHARED THE TRUTH ABOUT THE PRISON CAMPS.

124

THEY WERE LOCATED IN SWAMPS AND DESERTS, WHERE LIVING CONDITIONS WERE UNCOMFORTABLE AT BEST.

HOT COLD DUSTY

PEOPLE OFTEN LIVED IN CROWDED, UNSANITARY BUILDINGS, WITH NO RUNNING WATER.

AND THEY WEREN'T ALLOWED TO LEAVE.

THEY HADN'T BEEN CHARGED WITH ANY CRIME. SO THERE WAS NO WAY TO APPEAL.

ALL THEY COULD DO WAS WAIT—

THEY BUILT SCHOOLS AND PLACES TO WORSHIP.

THEY EVEN STARTED THEIR OWN NEWSPAPERS.

COUNCIL SOLE AUTHORITY—HEAD

POSTON DAILY Chronicle

THE ROHWER Outpost

Irrigator

Hunt Has Hot Water As Boilermen Return

MANZANAR FREE PRESS

DEFENDANTS GET $25 FINE

Will Be Shipping Furniture Soon

SCHOOL SITE SELECTED

By now, you might be remembering that Japan wasn't America's only enemy during World War II. The United States was also at war with Germany and Italy. So were Americans whose ancestors came from those countries rounded up and thrown in prison camps, too? Some were, but not on any large scale. While restrictions were placed on some Germans and Italians in the United States, there was no effort to round them up and remove them from their homes in great numbers. The government only did that to people of

Japanese descent. There were no prison camps full of German American or Italian American families and children.

Why the different treatment? Because of racism. Japanese Americans were a newer immigrant group than Germans and Italians. And they weren't white.

They'd faced prejudice from white people long before Pearl Harbor. The Japanese attack on American soil made it even worse. So even though America was at war with other nations, too, it was people of Japanese ancestry who were targeted. Most of those who faced imprisonment were forced to stay in the camps two to three years.

In 1943, attitudes began to change, and some prisoners were quietly let go. In June 1944, America's secretary of the interior, Harold Ickes, told President Roosevelt it was time to release everyone.

*I do say that the continued retention of these innocent people in the relocation centers would be a blot upon the history of this country.*

But Roosevelt wasn't ready to listen quite yet. There was an election coming up, and the president worried that people might not vote for him if he closed the prison camps. So he waited. In mid-December, after he'd been reelected, Roosevelt announced that the government had "carefully examined" all of those tens of thousands of Japanese Americans and decided they should be "allowed to enjoy the same privileges accorded other law-abiding American citizens or residents."

Finally, they were released! But Japanese Americans faced continued prejudice when they went home. And for many, home was simply gone. Some Japanese American families had friends who protected their property, but that was rare. More often, businesses and houses were lost. Farms were ruined. Beloved pets died because no one took care of them. The unfair imprisonment destroyed thousands of people's lives and futures.

Ickes was right when he told Roosevelt that the internment of Japanese Americans would be "a blot upon the history of this country." This chapter of American history is remembered today as a sad and shameful one.

# HAWAII'S HIDDEN PRISON CAMP

During World War II, hundreds of people of Japanese descent were imprisoned at a camp not far from Pearl Harbor. The Honouliuli prison camp was hot, muggy, and swarming with mosquitoes. It held both Japanese prisoners of war and American citizens who'd

A National Park Service photograph of Honouliuli Internment Camp from the 1940s

been forced to leave their homes. Japanese Americans weren't rounded up in huge numbers in Hawaii as they were on the mainland. Instead, officials targeted leaders of the Japanese community, such as teachers, business owners, and religious leaders. When the prison camp closed after the war, it quickly became overgrown with brush, and few people talked about it.

But in 1998, a TV station doing research contacted the Japanese Cultural Center on Oahu to ask about the camp. No one knew where it was, but after months of research, they were able to locate it, using clues from an old photograph.

Work began to uncover the prison camp's history, and in 2015, US President Barack Obama named the site a national monument—a reminder that freedom must always be protected in times of war.

# NINE
# AMERICA
# AT WAR

When America joined World War II, battles were already raging around the globe. Don't forget that the war was underway well before Pearl Harbor. By December 1941, Germany had already taken over Czechoslovakia, Poland, Denmark, Norway, Belgium, the Netherlands, Luxembourg, France, and the Soviet Union—and had attacked Britain as well. Italy had invaded Greece.

Japan had invaded China and French Indochina—and the day after Pearl Harbor, it bombed the Philippines, Wake Island, and Guam and invaded Thailand,

Malaya, and Hong Kong. By the end of the month, Japanese forces had also invaded Burma and Borneo.

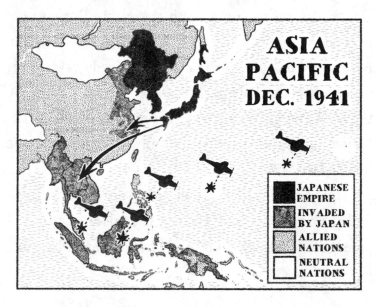

After the attack on Pearl Harbor, Americans from all different backgrounds enlisted in the military. World War II was before the civil rights movement, when new laws led to more equality for African Americans, so Black men weren't allowed to fight alongside white men, or even eat in the same mess halls.

They showed up to serve their country anyway. Many fixed planes, cooked food, or transported supplies. In March 1942, the United States activated the first all-Black unit of the Air Corps. The group, the 99th Pursuit Squadron, was made up of men from

African American pilots known as the Tuskegee Airmen talk after a day of fighting in the skies, in 1944.

the Tuskegee Institute training program and came to be known as the Tuskegee Airmen. During the war, African American pilots would fly more than a thousand missions in Europe and shoot down hundreds of enemy planes.

Native American men were also called on to serve in special roles during World War II. The military recruited men from several different tribes, including Comanches, Choctaws, Hopis, and Cherokees, to transmit messages in their tribal languages so they couldn't be decoded by the enemy. In 1941, the Marines

Navajo Code Talkers operate a portable radio set in a jungle clearing.

launched a program to recruit Navajo men as code talkers, to develop and memorize a special code for transmitting messages. Their work ended up saving thousands of lives during critical battles in the war.

Many Japanese American men wanted to enlist and help with the war effort, too. But they were left out. After Pearl Harbor, the US government had classified them as "enemy aliens," so they weren't allowed to enlist.

The year 1942 brought more setbacks for America and its allies. German U-boats began sinking tankers and cargo boats off America's East Coast. And in Europe, Nazi Germany's plans grew more sinister. The Wannsee Conference, a meeting of Nazi officials, outlined what they called the "Final Solution" for Jewish people in Europe. It was a plan to murder millions of people simply because they were Jewish. The Nazis ripped Jewish families from their homes and took them to concentration camps. Millions would be murdered in what is now known as the Holocaust. Others would be worked almost to death under terrible conditions. The rest of the world wouldn't understand the full extent of the horror until Allied soldiers marched into the camps near the end of the war.

Later in 1942, there were signs that the tide might be turning. By May, Japan had taken the Philippines, but the next month, Japan's navy was defeated at the Battle of Midway. Later that summer, Allied troops landed at Guadalcanal, in the Solomon Islands. It would take six months to secure the island, but it was clear that Japan was beginning to lose ground.

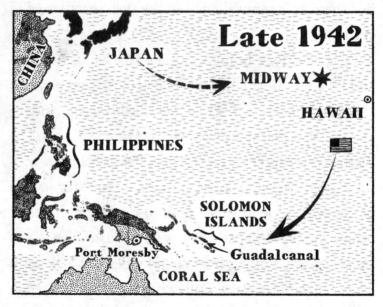

The same thing was true in Europe, where the Soviet Union was beating back German forces in the Battle of Stalingrad.

In November, the Allies attacked German and Italian forces in North Africa. This region was important because it was close to Italy and set the stage for the Allied invasion there.

But the victories came at a terrible cost. By the end of 1942, more than thirty-five thousand American servicemen had died. The United States needed more help on the battlefield.

Remember that policy that said Japanese Americans weren't allowed to sign on to fight for their country? In January 1943, President Roosevelt changed it, and they enlisted by the thousands. Twenty-five thousand Japanese Americans volunteered to fight for

America during World War II—including four thousand men who had been forced into those relocation camps. Their country had been treating them like second-class citizens, but they stepped up anyway—and turned out to be first-class soldiers.

Some were trained as linguists, or language experts. They served as translators and decoded important documents for America's military. They also helped with questioning prisoners and interpreting during battles.

Thousands more served in the 442nd Regimental Combat Team, a segregated unit made up of all Japanese American men that would distinguish itself during the war.

Some of the men in that unit started out as college students with the Reserve Officer Training Corps, or ROTC. After Pearl Harbor, ROTC students were called up to guard various locations around Oahu. Many of those ROTC students were Japanese Americans. When the government suddenly declared them "enemy aliens" who couldn't be part of America's military, they were sent back to campus.

An Oahu businessman and community leader

Members of the 442nd Regimental Combat Team
stand in formation at Hawaii's Iolani Palace, 1943.

named Hung Wai Ching saw how unfair that was. He
encouraged the young men to petition the government
to accept them as volunteers anyway. So that's what
the men did.

HAWAII IS OUR HOME; THE UNITED STATES OUR COUNTRY. WE KNOW BUT ONE LOYALTY AND THAT IS TO THE STARS AND STRIPES. WE WISH TO DO OUR PART AS LOYAL AMERICANS IN EVERY WAY POSSIBLE, AND WE HEREBY OFFER OURSELVES FOR WHATEVER SERVICE YOU MAY SEE FIT TO USE US.

That group of Japanese American college students became the Varsity Victory Volunteers, or Triple V. They were assigned to Schofield Barracks, divided into groups, and given different jobs. They cooked, paved roads, constructed buildings, and did all sorts of other work to help out. Ten months later, when the 442nd Regimental Combat Team was being formed, the men were invited to join.

That group of men who had at first been considered America's enemies went on to fight bravely in battles around the globe. The 442nd Regimental Combat Team earned more military medals and distinctions than any unit in US history. After the war, President Harry S. Truman honored the men with a Distinguished Unit Citation.

In July 1946, President Truman told the men of the 442nd Regimental Combat Team, "You fought, not only the enemy, but you fought prejudice, and you've won."

That moment with President Truman might make you think that the United States really appreciated and honored Japanese American soldiers. But their treatment during the war sometimes told a different story. Years after the war, secret documents came out that show Japanese American soldiers were used in a sort of failed experiment that was meant to train dogs to attack Japanese people.

## SECRET MILITARY MEMO

SUCCESSFUL RESULTS FROM THIS PROJECT CANNOT BE OBTAINED WITHOUT THE USE OF AT LEAST TWELVE JAPANESE-AMERICANS AS ASSISTANT TRAINERS AND [IT IS] REQUESTED THAT SUCH PERSONNEL BE MADE AVAILABLE. THESE TRAINERS WOULD BE USED AS "BAIT" FOR THE DOGS.

SO IN OCTOBER 1942, TWENTY-FIVE JAPANESE AMERICAN SOLDIERS WERE CHOSEN FOR A SECRET TRAINING MISSION ON REMOTE CAT ISLAND, IN MISSISSIPPI.

THEIR MISSION WAS TO TRAIN DOGS TO RECOGNIZE AND ATTACK JAPANESE PEOPLE.

BACK THEN, THE ARMY BELIEVED THAT JAPANESE PEOPLE HAD A DISTINCTIVE SCENT. THEY DON'T. BUT THAT WAS THE IDEA BEHIND THE PROGRAM.

CAT ISLAND WAS CHOSEN AS THE SITE FOR THE TRAINING BECAUSE IT WAS SIMILAR TO SOME OF THE PACIFIC ISLANDS WHERE THE WAR WAS TAKING PLACE.

THE DOGS IN THE PROGRAM WERE PETS THAT PEOPLE HAD DONATED TO THE US MILITARY.

THEY DIDN'T KNOW HOW THEIR PETS WERE GOING TO BE USED.

ONCE ON THE ISLAND, JAPANESE AMERICAN SOLDIERS WERE GIVEN SOME BASIC PROTECTION—

NECK GUARDS, FACE MASKS, BURLAP SACKS, AND HOCKEY GLOVES.

SOLDIERS WERE ORDERED TO TRAIN THE DOGS TO RECOGNIZE AND ATTACK JAPANESE PEOPLE.

—RAY NOSAKA, 100TH INFANTRY BATTALION

THEY SAID TO "TRAIN THE DOGS," BUT WE CALLED IT "DOG BAIT."

WE WERE THE BAIT.

THE GOAL? TURN THE DOGS INTO WEAPONS OF WAR.

SOMETIMES THE SOLDIERS WERE ORDERED TO FALL DOWN SO THE DOGS COULD BITE THEM.

SOMETIMES THEY WERE ORDERED TO HIT DOGS THAT WERE TIED TO THE FENCE.

THEN THE DOGS WOULD BE RELEASED WITH AN ORDER TO ATTACK THE SOLDIERS.

KILL 'EM!

EVENTUALLY, THE DOGS WERE PULLED AWAY.
BUT NOT ALWAYS BEFORE THE MEN WERE HURT.

THEY'D BE TAKEN FOR MEDICAL
TREATMENT AND THEN SENT BACK.

SOMETIMES SOLDIERS WERE
ORDERED TO HIDE IN THE
ISLAND'S SWAMP. . . .

IT WAS HOT, MUGGY, AND
BUZZING WITH MOSQUITOES.

THE MEN WOULD
CLING TO THE TREES,

WITH VICIOUS DOGS AND HUNGRY
ALLIGATORS WAITING BELOW.

The top-secret experiment failed in less than four months. Documents show that the US military knew from the start it would be a huge problem if people found out about it.

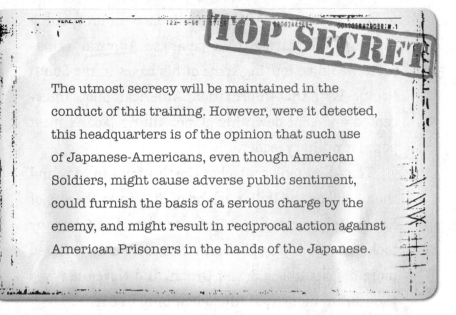

The utmost secrecy will be maintained in the conduct of this training. However, were it detected, this headquarters is of the opinion that such use of Japanese-Americans, even though American Soldiers, might cause adverse public sentiment, could furnish the basis of a serious charge by the enemy, and might result in reciprocal action against American Prisoners in the hands of the Japanese.

In other words, if anyone finds out about this, the public will be really upset. Also, American prisoners of war might end up being treated the same way we're treating these poor soldiers.

None of that kept the military from launching the program. It just made them work extra hard to keep it a secret.

Despite the way they were treated, Japanese American soldiers continued to serve with honor, and the war raged on. In March 1943, America won control of New Guinea in the Battle of the Bismarck Sea. The following month, Allied intelligence intercepted a message and learned that Japanese Admiral Yamamoto would be touring some of his bases in the South Pacific. With that information, American pilots intercepted and shot down his plane, killing Japan's most popular military leader.

The Allies took control of North Africa in May and then bombed the Italian island of Sicily and the city of Rome. Italy surrendered in September, but Germany took over the fighting. Meanwhile, Germany suffered more defeats in the Soviet Union, and November was the start of months of Allied bombing in Berlin.

Allied bombings inflicted heavy damage in Berlin, Germany.

In 1944, major battles raged in both Europe and the Pacific, including the invasion we now know as D-Day. On the morning of June 6, 1944, thousands of Allied paratroopers dropped into Nazi-occupied France, behind enemy lines in Normandy. At the same time, more than five thousand Allied ships were crossing the English Channel to launch an invasion with more then 150,000 troops. They landed on the shores of Normandy and fought their way up the beaches to begin taking France back from the Nazis.

As German forces retreated, Japan was losing ground in the Pacific. The same month as D-Day,

Allied troops come ashore in Normandy on D-Day.

US Marines invaded Saipan, and the Battle of the Philippine Sea was raging, too. Vice Admiral Jisaburo Ozawa told his men the fate of the Japanese empire rested on this battle and urged them to give all they had. But in the end, the US Navy would defeat the Japanese Combined Fleet. By mid-July, Allied troops had secured Saipan as well.

If you're starting to feel like there was a lot going on in a lot of different places during World War II, you're absolutely right. While all of this was happening in the Pacific, other Allied troops were pushing farther

Allied bombings destroyed most of the historic German city of Dresden in 1945.

into France. They freed Paris from Nazi control on August 25 and went on to battle Germany on its own turf. Those battles raged into the winter. In February 1945, nine hundred British and American bombers hit the German city of Dresden and set off a firestorm that killed thirty-five thousand civilians.

That April, American and Soviet forces came together to cut Germany in half. Surrounded, and with the Soviets pushing into Berlin, Nazi leader Adolf Hitler killed himself in a bunker. Finally, on May 7, 1945, Germany surrendered, and there were celebrations all over Europe. It was known as Victory in Europe Day, or V-E Day for short.

A V-E Day celebration in London

But the war in the Pacific wasn't finished yet. Allied forces had taken back the Philippines in a huge sea battle that marked the end of the Japanese Navy. In February 1945, US Marines had invaded the Japanese island of Iwo Jima, eventually capturing it after a month of fighting.

# CAPTURING A MOMENT (THE SECOND TIME AROUND)

This image of US Marines raising the American flag on Iwo Jima became one of the most famous photographs in American history. Photographer Joe Rosenthal snapped the famous photo, but it doesn't tell the whole story of what happened that day. The truth is, the American flag was already flying when Rosenthal showed up with his camera.

Another photographer, Marine Sergeant Louis Lowery, was on top of Iwo Jima's Mount Suribachi when American Marines raised the first flag after their victory. He took this photo of the moment.

Not long after Lowery got the shot, American soldiers below spotted the flag and started celebrating with whistles and gunshots. Then there was a brief firefight with Japanese forces at the top of the mountain, and Lowery had to run for cover. He ended up falling and smashing his camera, so he headed down the mountain for new equipment.

Famed photographer Joe Rosenthal was just on his way up. Lowery let him know he was too late—the flag was already up. But Rosenthal kept going to see the view from the top. When he got there, he found some Marines

UNITED STATES POSTAGE

3¢

IWO JIMA

getting ready to put up a second flag. They were replacing that first flag with a bigger one that would be easier to see from below.

Rosenthal may have missed the shot the first time, but he wasn't about to miss it again.

He got himself into position and took the photo—and it turned out really great. So great, in fact, that Lowery's photo of the first flag being raised never got much attention when it was released later on. It was Rosenthal's photo of the replacement flag that ended up being the inspiration for a postage stamp and a national monument.

Battles raged on the Pacific front through the spring of 1945. In March, America bombed Japanese cities, killing at least eighty thousand people and destroying a million people's homes. In April, Allied forces took the Japanese city of Okinawa. That summer, two months after Germany had surrendered, at a meeting called the Potsdam Conference, American, English, and Chinese leaders proclaimed that Japan would have to surrender, or face "utter destruction." Japan said no.

A week later, on August 6, 1945, America dropped the world's first atomic bomb on the Japanese city of Hiroshima. An atomic bomb is a super-powerful

Atomic bomb cloud over the Japanese city of Hiroshima, 1945

weapon that uses nuclear energy to create a massive explosion. The bomb that fell on Hiroshima killed at least eighty thousand men, women, and children instantly. Another hundred thousand later died from radiation poisoning, a sickness caused by the fallout of that kind of bomb.

Japan still refused to surrender, and on August 9,

America dropped another atomic bomb. This one hit the city of Nagasaki, killing more than seventy thousand people. Six days later, Japan surrendered and the war was finally over. By then, it had lost every one of the aircraft carriers and battleships that had been involved in the bombing of Pearl Harbor.

Japan signed the surrender document on board the USS *Missouri* in Tokyo Bay. Among the American warships nearby was the USS *West Virginia,* one of the American battleships that had been attacked at Pearl Harbor.

Japan's foreign affairs minister signs surrender papers on board the USS *Missouri* on September 2, 1945.

## TEN
## TIME TO REMEMBER, TIME TO HEAL

Today, America observes December 7 as National Pearl Harbor Remembrance Day to honor the 2,335 servicemen and sixty-eight civilians who died in the attack. The tradition goes back to 1994, when President Bill Clinton issued a proclamation for the observance, but those who lost friends and loved ones at Pearl Harbor have been remembering much longer than that.

In 1958, President Dwight D. Eisenhower declared Pearl Harbor a national monument, and the nation made plans to build a memorial over the remains of the USS *Arizona*.

The sinking of the USS *Arizona*

After the attack on Pearl Harbor, parts of the USS *Arizona* were salvaged and used in the war effort. The navy recovered machinery, guns, and ammunition. But the rest was left submerged in about forty feet of water—a final resting place for more than nine hundred sailors who went down with their ship.

When the decision was made to build a memorial over the wreckage, the government didn't set aside any money for the project. Instead, the plan was to pay for it through donations. Elvis Presley, who was a big

rock-and-roll star back then, held a fundraiser at Bloch Arena—the same building where the bands had battled it out the night before the attack. It raised more than $60,000 to go toward the half-million-dollar project.

At first, the government wasn't sure exactly what kind of memorial should be built. The navy put out a request for bids, which meant that different people could submit their ideas. The navy had said that the memorial should be "something like a bridge, and it had to be able to hold at least 200 people." A man named Alfred Preis ended up submitting the winning design.

ALFRED PREIS WAS BORN IN AUSTRIA, WHERE HE STUDIED ARCHITECTURE AS A YOUNG MAN.

HE GOT MARRIED IN MARCH 1938 . . .

. . . BUT THE JOY OF THAT DAY WAS OVERSHADOWED BY FEAR.

THE NAZIS HAD JUST SWEPT INTO AUSTRIA.

PREIS WAS CATHOLIC, BUT HIS FATHER WAS JEWISH. HE KNEW HIS FAMILY WAS IN DANGER.

SO HE AND HIS NEW WIFE MADE PLANS TO FLEE.

THANKS TO AN ORGANIZATION THAT HELPED REFUGEES, THE COUPLE WAS ABLE TO ESCAPE AND SETTLE IN HONOLULU.

BUT JUST TWO YEARS LATER,

THE JAPANESE ATTACKED PEARL HARBOR.

FOREIGNERS ON OAHU WERE IMMEDIATELY TREATED WITH SUSPICION. JAPANESE PEOPLE ESPECIALLY, BUT ALSO SOME GERMANS AND AUSTRIANS.

PREIS WAS HELD AT THE SAND ISLAND PRISON CAMP FOR THREE MONTHS.

YOU MIGHT THINK HE'D BE TOO ANGRY ABOUT THAT TO CONSIDER SUBMITTING A DESIGN, BUT PREIS HAD A VISION FOR THE USS ARIZONA MEMORIAL:

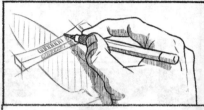

A 184-FOOT STRUCTURE MADE OF WHITE CONCRETE AND STEEL, TO BE BUILT OVER THE WRECKAGE OF THE SUNKEN BATTLESHIP FORTY FEET BELOW.

IT WOULD HAVE THREE MAIN AREAS, STARTING WITH THE ENTRY ROOM.

THEN THERE WAS AN ASSEMBLY HALL WITH TWENTY-ONE OPEN-AIR WINDOWS.

THE FLOOR IN THE ASSEMBLY HALL WAS SOLID, BUT WITH A HOLE CUT THROUGH IT, SO PEOPLE COULD LOOK DOWN TO THE WRECK BELOW.

THE THIRD ROOM WOULD BE THE SHRINE . . .

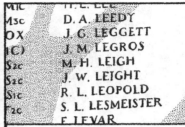

MIC   H. L. LEE
M3c   D. A. LEEDY
OX    J. G. LEGGETT
1C)   J. M. LEGROS
S2c   M. H. LEIGH
S2c   J. W. LEIGHT
S1c   R. L. LEOPOLD
2c    S. L. LESMEISTER
      E. LEVAR

. . . WITH THE NAMES OF ALL THOSE WHO HAD DIED ON THE SHIP.

WHEN THE MEMORIAL WAS FIRST BUILT, SOME PEOPLE DIDN'T LIKE THE DESIGN. BUT PREIS SAID THE MEMORIAL'S SHAPE WAS SYMBOLIC.

ITS SAGGING MIDDLE REPRESENTED AMERICA'S LOW POINT AFTER THE PEARL HARBOR ATTACK,

WHILE ITS UPLIFTED ENDS SYMBOLIZED AMERICAN PRIDE AND ULTIMATE VICTORY IN THE WAR.

CONSTRUCTION ON THE MEMORIAL BEGAN IN 1960. IT WAS DEDICATED WITH A CEREMONY ON MAY 30, 1962.

TODAY, THE USS ARIZONA MEMORIAL WELCOMES ABOUT 1.8 MILLION VISITORS EVERY YEAR.

MANY DON'T REALIZE THAT THE ARCHITECT OF THIS AMERICAN MONUMENT WAS AN IMMIGRANT WHO WAS HIMSELF A VICTIM OF THE FEAR AND IGNORANCE THAT COST SO MANY INNOCENT PEOPLE THEIR FREEDOM AFTER THE PEARL HARBOR ATTACK.

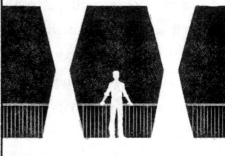

USS *Arizona* Memorial

The USS *Arizona* Memorial honors the 1,177 sailors who died when their ship was attacked. Even today, the battleship's hull is a tomb for more than nine hundred men whose bodies were never recovered. The National Historic Landmarks also include memorials for the 429 men who died when the USS *Oklahoma* capsized and the fifty-eight who were killed on the USS *Utah*.

# AN ENVIRONMENTAL CHALLENGE

When the USS *Arizona* sank, its hull was full of oil. Ever since then, that oil had been slowly leaking out of the ship and into the ocean. The droplets rise to the surface to create pools. Some veterans say it looks as if the battleship is crying black tears. It's an emotional sight, but the leaking oil is also a concern for the environment.

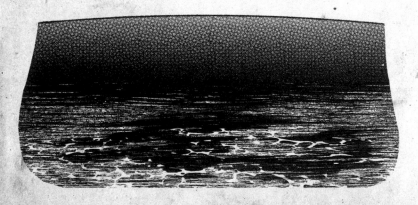

The problem with having an underwater memorial like the USS *Arizona* is that seawater corrodes metal. The battleship won't last forever, and the oil leak is likely to get worse as the ship ages. It's a tough situation because the oil is stored in multiple places on the ship. It would be hard to deal with the oil without damaging the ship and disturbing the grave site. The navy and the National Park Service estimate that the USS *Arizona* leaks two to nine quarts of oil each day. They're doing studies now to figure out how quickly the oil might become a more serious problem, and what can be done about it.

Many of those who survived the attack on Pearl Harbor have returned to Oahu each December to remember and honor those who died. But America's World War II veterans are old now, and every year, there are fewer veterans left.

HERBERT BUEHL, WHO DIED IN 2002, WENT TO PEARL HARBOR IN 1996 FOR THE FIFTY-FIFTH ANNIVERSARY OF THE ATTACK.

HE REMEMBERED THAT MORNING. . . .

BUEHL WAS GETTING READY FOR CHURCH SERVICES WHEN THE FIRST BOMBS DROPPED.

HE RAN TO HIS BATTLE STATION ON THE USS ARIZONA.

THEN THERE WAS AN ENORMOUS EXPLOSION, "JUST LIKE A TORNADO HAD GONE THROUGH THE SHIP."

THE BLAST KNOCKED BUEHL DOWN A LADDER.

WHEN HE CLIMBED UP, HE FOUND THE FRONT PART OF THE SHIP BURNING.

HE AND SOME OTHERS REALIZED THEY'D HAVE TO ABANDON SHIP.

OIL COVERED THE WATER AND MADE IT ALMOST IMPOSSIBLE TO SWIM.

BUEHL SWAM TO A CEMENT QUAY, WHERE SOME OTHER SAILORS PULLED HIM FROM THE WATER.

FROM THERE, THEY TOOK A SMALL MOTORBOAT TO FORD ISLAND AS THE JAPANESE PLANES FIRED DOWN FROM THE SKY.

IT ALL HAPPENED SO FAST.

BUEHL NEVER GOT TO SAY GOODBYE TO THE FRIENDS HE LOST THAT DAY.

ON THE FIFTY-FIFTH ANNIVERSARY OF THE ATTACK, HE WENT UP TO THE PUNCHBOWL CEMETERY FOR A SERVICE TO HONOR HIS FELLOW SAILORS WHO DIED.

"JUST BEFORE THE SERVICE WAS OVER, IT RAINED. . . . IT WAS JUST A MIST, BUT IT WAS JUST LIKE TEARS FROM HEAVEN. THAT THESE MEN REMEMBERED US, TOO."

Surviving members of the USS *Arizona* crew can choose to have their remains interred on the ship when they die. After a ceremony, the veteran's ashes are given to divers, who swim the urn into the USS *Arizona*'s gun turret four and place it into a slot, where it slides into the ship. That way, the men are able to share the final resting place of their fellow sailors who died in the attack.

This is an honor reserved only for those who were USS *Arizona* crew members at the time of the attack. But any Pearl Harbor survivor can choose to have their ashes scattered over the place in the harbor where their ship was moored that morning.

## REMEMBERING HIROSHIMA

Across the Pacific Ocean, there is a different memorial—in Hiroshima, where that first atomic bomb was dropped, killing so many Japanese families. The Hiroshima Peace Memorial, the Genbaku Dome, was the only structure in the city center that survived the

1945 bombing. It's been preserved as a reminder of what happened when America
dropped the most powerful bomb ever created
on a city full of civilians. The memorial ex-
presses hope for world peace.

Hirsoshima Peace Memorial

Nearby in Peace Memorial Park, a flame of
peace has burned since 1964. The memorial
flame will continue to burn until nuclear
weapons are eliminated around the world.

Japanese American families also remember the hardship they endured in the years that followed the attack on Pearl Harbor. Many years later, America acknowledged what a mistake it was to send all of those innocent people to prison camps. In 1982, a congressional commission issued a report on the treatment of Japanese Americans after Pearl Harbor. It said, "The broad historical causes which shaped these decisions were race prejudice, war hysteria, and a failure of political leadership."

In 1988, America officially apologized for the prison camps. Two years later, Congress started paying reparations to survivors of the camps, giving back some of the $1.6 billion lost when people were forced to sell their homes and businesses so quickly.

In 2001, Congress voted to make ten internment sites historic landmarks. The Japanese American Citizens League fought for that so the former camps would "forever stand as reminders that this nation failed in its most sacred duty to protect its citizens against prejudice, greed, and political expediency."

The prior year, the National Japanese American Memorial to Patriotism had opened in Washington, DC.

National Japanese American Memorial to Patriotism

It includes a bronze statue of two cranes trying to free themselves from barbed wire. Behind that sculpture is a wall engraved with the history of the Japanese in wartime and the names of those who died in World War II.

America and Japan were fierce enemies throughout World War II, but today the two nations are allies and friends. Both nations remember the past and have taken steps to heal. In 2016, President Barack Obama became the first American president to visit Hiroshima.

*"SEVENTY-ONE YEARS AGO, ON A BRIGHT CLOUDLESS MORNING, DEATH FELL FROM THE SKY AND THE WORLD WAS CHANGED."*
*—PRESIDENT BARACK OBAMA*

Hiroshima Peace Memorial Park

Later that year, Prime Minster Shinzo Abe of Japan visited Pearl Harbor.

*"WE MUST NEVER REPEAT THE HORRORS OF WAR AGAIN. THIS IS THE SOLEMN VOW WE, THE PEOPLE OF JAPAN, HAVE TAKEN."*
*—PRIME MINISTER SHINZO ABE*

Neither leader apologized for what their countries did during World War II, but both promised to work toward a better future.

# A WORLD WAR II AND PEARL HARBOR TIMELINE

**1924**—US Army officer William Mitchell tours the Pacific and Far East and warns that Japan's plans to expand its empire might lead to war with the United States, and that it could begin with surprise attacks on Pearl Harbor and the Philippines.

**1931**—Japan invades Manchuria, which is part of China.

**1937**—Japan launches a full-scale invasion of China. The United States sends relief funds to China but doesn't get involved in fighting.

**1938**—A US War Department survey warns that Japan might stage a surprise attack on Pearl Harbor someday.

**1939**—Nazi Germany invades Czechoslovakia and Poland. France and Britain declare war on Germany.

The Soviet Union invades Poland and Finland.

**1940**—US President Franklin Delano Roosevelt orders the US Pacific Fleet from San Diego, where it's been stationed, to Pearl Harbor as a show of force to Japan.

Germany invades Denmark, Norway, Luxembourg, the Netherlands, France, and Belgium.

Italy joins Germany and declares war on Britain and France.

Germany begins bombing Great Britain.

Japan, which has been trying to expand its territory, invades French Indochina and joins Germany and Italy in the Tripartite Pact, which promises that if any of those nations are attacked, the other two will come to its defense.

American intelligence officers crack the code used to send messages to Japanese diplomats.

Italy invades Greece.

**1941**

**January**—Admiral Isoroku Yamamoto of Japan begins work on a plan to attack Pearl Harbor.

The American ambassador to Japan, Joseph Grew, hears about the plan and sends a cable to Washington.

US Navy Secretary Frank Knox writes a letter to Secretary of War Henry Stimson to alert him that a Japanese attack is a possibility. Knox promises that the military will take another look at whether it is prepared.

**February**—Admiral Husband E. Kimmel is appointed commander of the Pacific Fleet at Pearl Harbor.

Lieutenant General Walter C. Short takes command of the US Army's Hawaiian Department.

**March**—Army and navy commanders write a memo with a plan to defend Oahu, suggesting air patrols.

**June**—Germany invades the Soviet Union.

**Summer**—Commander Minoru Genda is put in charge of preparing men to carry out the Japanese attack on Pearl Harbor and trains his pilots at Kagoshima Bay in southern Japan.

**September**—American intelligence officers intercept a message and learn that Japan is looking for information about the location of battleships at Pearl Harbor.

**November**—Japanese aircraft carriers set out for Hawaii, even though Japan's ambassadors are in Washington, talking with US officials to try to avoid a military conflict.

America demands that Japan withdraw all of its troops from China.

Secretary of State Cordell Hull obtains a speech from the Japanese prime minister, Hideki Tojo, and believes that war might be imminent. Hull calls Roosevelt on vacation in Georgia, and the president returns to Washington.

**December 1**—Emperor Hirohito and Prime Minister Tojo give final approval for Japan's attack on Pearl Harbor.

**December 2**—Admiral Kimmel asks for an update on Japan's aircraft carriers and learns that some are missing.

**December 3**—American intelligence officials intercept more Japanese messages that suggest war might be imminent.

**December 6**—President Roosevelt reads an intercepted memo sent from Tokyo to the Japanese embassy in the United States and says, "This means war." He sends a letter to Emperor Hirohito to try to prevent war, but the letter isn't delivered until it's too late.

**December 7**—Japanese planes take off from their aircraft carriers before dawn and arrive in Oahu to attack Pearl Harbor, devastating the Pacific Fleet and killing more than 2,400 people.

**December 8**—The United States declares war on Japan.

Japan attacks the Philippines, Wake Island, Guam, Thailand, Malaya, and Hong Kong.

**December 11**—Italy and Germany declare war on the United States, and the United States declares war on those two nations as well.

## 1942

**January**—German U-boats sink twenty-five tankers off America's eastern seaboard.

Nazi leaders at the Wannsee Conference outline the "Final Solution," a plan to murder millions of Jewish people in Europe.

**February**—President Roosevelt issues Executive Order 9066, which results in tens of thousands of Japanese Americans being removed from their homes and sent to prison camps.

**March**—The United States activates the first all-Black unit of the Air Corps, which will later come to be known as the Tuskegee Airmen.

**June**—Allied forces defeat Japan at the Battle of Midway.

**November**—Allied forces defeat German and Italian forces in North Africa in Operation Torch.

## 1943

**February**—President Roosevelt changes America's policy so Japanese Americans are allowed to serve in combat. They enlist by the thousands, volunteering to fight for their country.

**March**—American forces take control of New Guinea in the Battle of the Bismarck Sea.

**April**—American intelligence officers intercept a message and learn that Yamamoto will be touring bases in the South Pacific. With this information, US pilots intercept his flight and shoot down his plane.

**July**—Allied forces bomb Sicily and Rome.

**September**—Italy surrenders to Allied forces. Germany takes over the fighting in Italy.

**October**—Italy declares war on Germany, officially switching sides in the war.

**November**—Allied planes begin the bombing of Berlin.

## 1944

**June**—Allied paratroopers drop into Nazi-occupied France, and thousands of ships cross the English Channel to launch the D-Day invasion of Normandy, beginning a push to take France back from the Nazis.

US Marines invade the Japanese island of Saipan.

America's navy defeats Japan's in the Battle of the Philippine Sea. Japan's navy suffers major losses.

**August**—Allied troops free Paris from Nazi control and push into Germany.

## 1945

**February**—British and American planes bomb the German city of Dredsen, killing 35,000 civilians.

US Marines invade and eventually capture the island of Iwo Jima.

**March**—America drops napalm bombs on Japanese cities, killing at least 80,000 people.

**April**—Allied forces invade the Japanese island of Okinawa.

American and Soviet forces combine to cut Germany in half. Surrounded, Nazi leader Adolf Hitler kills himself in a bunker.

**May**—Germany surrenders.

**July–August**—Allied leaders meet at the Potsdam Conference and proclaim that Japan must surrender unconditionally or face "utter destruction." Japan refuses.

**August 6**—America drops the world's first atomic bomb on Hiroshima, killing more than 80,000 people instantly, along with another 100,000 who would later die from radiation poisoning.

**August 9**—America drops an atomic bomb on Nagasaki, killing more than 70,000 people.

**August 15**—Japan surrenders. The formal surrender document is signed in September on board the USS *Missouri* in Tokyo Bay, and World War II is over.

**1958**—US President Dwight D. Eisenhower gives approval for the creation of the USS *Arizona* Memorial.

**1962**—The USS *Arizona* Memorial is dedicated.

**1966**—Hiroshima's city council passes a resolution to create the Hiroshima Peace Memorial, permanently preserving the Genbaku Dome, the only building left standing in the city center after the 1945 atomic bomb was dropped there.

**1982**—A US congressional commission issues a report on the internment of Japanese Americans following Pearl Harbor, blaming "race prejudice, war hysteria, and a failure of political leadership" for the shameful policy.

**1988**—America officially apologizes for the imprisonment of Japanese Americans.

**1990**—The US Congress begins paying $1.6 billion in reparations to survivors of prison camps.

**1994**—US President Bill Clinton issues a proclamation to make December 7 National Pearl Harbor Remembrance Day.

**2001**—Congress votes to make ten Japanese internment sites historic landmarks.

The Japanese American Memorial to Patriotism opens in Washington, DC.

**2016**—Barack Obama becomes the first US president to visit Hiroshima.

Prime Minister Shinzo Abe of Japan visits Pearl Harbor.

# AUTHOR'S NOTE

When I was in elementary school, I remember reading in my social studies book about the Japanese attack on Pearl Harbor and how it brought the United States into World War II. But it wasn't until I was older that I learned about how people of Japanese ancestry were treated during that time period. The racism and fear that led to the imprisonment of Japanese Americans isn't a part of history that makes Americans proud. For a long time, it was left out of history books and social studies classes. But today, most Americans realize that chapter in our history is too important to forget. When a nation won't talk about its failures, it's likely to make the same mistakes again and again.

Even today, some political leaders suggest that it might be a good idea to round up groups of people from certain minority groups to restrict their freedom. When those conversations begin, other leaders are quick to remind them of the shameful legacy of the treatment of Japanese Americans after Pearl Harbor. It's not a story that paints America in a flattering light, but it's an important one to remember.

Today, the story of Japanese Americans is included in films and displays at the Pearl Harbor Visitor Center. I spent time there in December 2018, when I was doing research for this book, and had the opportunity to see the USS *Arizona* Memorial from a tour boat. The memorial was closed at the time due to repair work, but National Park Service guides were still available to tell the battleship's story and answer questions.

I also had the chance to talk with Pearl Harbor survivor Everett Hyland that day. He was eighteen years old and serving as a member of the antenna repair squad on the USS *Pennsylvania* when Pearl Harbor was attacked. As soon as the bombing started, Hyland fell into line carrying ammunition out to the antiaircraft guns. He was wounded when a bomb exploded near his battle station, but he made it off the ship and got medical treatment. Nine months later, he returned to service on the USS *Memphis*. He was awarded a Purple Heart for his courage and sacrifice. When he retired from the military, he became a science teacher.

Hyland was ninety-five years old when I met him, and still spending time at the Pearl Harbor National Memorial to meet visitors from all over the world. He and many other survivors of Pearl Harbor continue to tell their stories so that this moment in history—and all that it meant for the world—will never be forgotten.

If you'd like to learn more about Pearl Harbor, the imprisonment of Japanese Americans, and World War II, here are some books, websites, and museums to explore:

## BOOKS

*Farewell to Manzanar* by Jeanne Wakatsuki Houston and James D. Houston (Houghton Mifflin Harcourt, reprint edition, 2017)

*Heroes of Pearl Harbor* (10 True Tales) by Allen Zullo (Scholastic, 2016)

*Imprisoned: The Betrayal of Japanese Americans During World War II* by Martin W. Sandler (Bloomsbury, 2013)

*Remember Pearl Harbor: American and Japanese Survivors Tell Their Stories* (National Geographic, 2015)

*Sachiko: A Nagasaki Bomb Survivor's Story* by Caren Stelson (Lerner, 2016)

# WEBSITES

*Fighting for the Right to Fight: African American Experiences in World War II* is a special exhibit with oral histories, profile panels, and artifacts from the National World War II Museum in New Orleans: righttofightexhibit.org

*Japanese American Incarceration in World War II*, a free curriculum unit on the website of the Choices Program, affiliated with the Department of History at Brown University, has interviews, videos, maps, and other resources: choices.edu/curriculum-unit /japanese-american-incarceration-world-war-ii

The Pearl Harbor National Memorial website from the National Park Service has information on visiting this historic site in Oahu, as well as lots of resources for learning more: nps.gov/valr

# MUSEUMS TO VISIT

Hiroshima Peace Memorial (Hiroshima, Japan)

Japanese American National Museum (Los Angeles, CA)

National WWII Museum (New Orleans, LA)

Pearl Harbor National Memorial (Honolulu, HI)

# BIBLIOGRAPHY

Bauernfeind, Ingo W. *USS* Arizona: *The Enduring Legacy of a Battleship.* Mülheim, Germany: Bauernfeind Press, 2018. Kindle.

Clarke, Thurston. *Pearl Harbor Ghosts: The Legacy of December 7, 1941.* New York: Ballantine Books, 1991.

Editors of *Life. Pearl Harbor 75 Years Later: A Day of Infamy and Its Legacy.* New York: Time Inc. Books, 2016.

"Establishment of the Honouliuli National Monument." Proclamation No. 9234. 80 Fed. Reg. 11067. February 24, 2015. federalregister.gov/documents/2015/02/27/2015-04352 /establishment-of-the-honouliuli-national-monument.

Frail, T. A. "American Incarceration: The Injustice of Japanese-American Internment Camps Resonates Strongly to This Day." *Smithsonian,* January 2017. smithsonianmag.com/history /injustice-japanese-americans-internment-camps-resonates -strongly-180961422.

Goddard, Jacqui. "Pearl Harbour Memo Shows US Warned of Japanese Attack." *Telegraph* (UK). December 4, 2011. telegraph.co.uk/news /worldnews/northamerica/usa/8932197/Pearl-Harbour-memo -shows-US-warned-of-Japanese-attack.html.

Hawaii Nisei Story: Americans of Japanese Ancestry During WWII. "Ray Nosaka's Story." nisei.hawaii.edu/object/io_1153256967265.

Hawai'i Volcanoes National Park. "The Untold Story: Internment of Japanese Americans in Hawai'i." Documentary, 2012. nps.gov /media/video/view.htm?id=293C7818-DFB2-563E-97F5763 EB6258BA3

Ho'okele Staff. "Jitterbug champ recalls historic Battle of the Bands." *Ho'okele Pearl Harbor–Hickam News*. December 16, 2016. hookelenews.com/jitterbug-champ-recalls-historic-battle -of-the-bands.

Hyland, Everett. Personal interview. December 23, 2018.

Japanese American Military History Collective, Go for Broke National Education Center Oral History Project. "Ray Nosaka Oral History Interview Transcript (Full Interview), October 19, 1998." ndajams.omeka.net/items/show/1053068.

Jasper, Joy Waldron, James P. Delgado, and Jim Adams. *The USS Arizona: The Ship, the Men, the Pearl Harbor Attack, and the Symbol that Aroused America*. New York: St. Martin's Press, 2001.

Jones, Meg. "75 Years Later, USS *Arizona* Band Remembered." *Milwaukee Journal Sentinel*. December 6, 2016. jsonline.com /story/news/special-reports/pearl-harbor/2016/12/06/75-years -later-uss-arizona-band-remembered/94626818.

Lee, James. Personal interview with author. December 23, 2018.

Luksovsky, Katrina R. *Ford Island, December 7, 1941: A Collection of Eyewitness Accounts from the Residents Closest to Battleship Row*. Rev. ed. Self-published, CreateSpace, 2016.

McWilliams, Bill. *Sunday in Hell: Pearl Harbor Minute by Minute.* New York: Open Road, 2014.

National Museum of the American Indian, Smithsonian. "Native Words, Native Warriors—Code Talking: Intelligence and Bravery." americanindian.si.edu/education/codetalkers/html/chapter4 .html.

National Museum of the US Air Force. "Brig. Gen. William 'Billy' Mitchell." April 9, 2015. www.nationalmuseum.af.mil/Visit /Museum-Exhibits/Fact-Sheets/Display/Article/196418/brig -gen-william-billy-mitchell.

National Museum of the US Air Force. "Lt. Phillip Rasmussen and His P-36A." April 29, 2015. www.nationalmuseum.af.mil/Visit /Museum-Exhibits/Fact-Sheets/Display/Article/195995/lt -phillip-rasmussen-and-his-p-36a.

National Park Service Pearl Harbor National Memorial. "Oral History Interviews." Accessed August 23, 2019. nps.gov/valr/learn /historyculture/oral-history-interviews.htm.

*A. H. Mortensen, USS* Oklahoma

*Albert Luco Fickel, USS* Pennsylvania

*Amy Kimura (both interviews)*

*Bill Guerin, USS* Arizona

*C. E. Thompson, assistant fire chief at navy yard*

*Clark Simmons, USS* Utah

*Clinton Westbrook, USS* Arizona

*Donald Stratton, USS* Arizona *(both interviews)*

*Etsuo Sayama, US Engineer Department (three interviews)*

*Glen Lane, USS* Arizona *(both interviews)*

*Harriet Kuwamoto (three interviews)*

*Harry Goda*

*Jim Green, USS* Arizona

*Jim Miller, USS* Arizona

*John Anderson, USS* Arizona

*John W. Evans, USS* Arizona

*John David Harris, USS* Arizona

*Michael M. Ganitch, USS* Pennsylvania

*John Harry "Jack" McCarron, USS* Arizona

*Milton Tom Hurst, USS* Arizona

*Loraine Yamada (both interviews)*

*Ralph William Landreth, USS* Arizona

*Masao Asada (both interviews)*

*Ruth Yamaguchi (five interviews)*

Patterson, Thom. "The Inside Story of the Famous Iwo Jima Photo." CNN. Updated February 23, 2016. cnn.com/2015/02/22/world /cnnphotos-iwo-jima.

Pearl Harbor Visitors Bureau. "USS *Pennsylvania:* The Day the Music Died." Accessed August 26, 2019. visitpearlharbor.org/uss -pennsylvania-day-music-died.

Prange, Gordon W. *At Dawn We Slept: The Untold Story of Pearl Harbor.* New York: Penguin, 1982.

Sharp, Rebecca K. "How an Eagle Feels When His Wings Are Clipped and Caged: Relocation Center Newspapers Describe Japanese American Internment in World War II." National Archives. *Prologue* 41, no. 4, Genealogy Notes (Winter 2009). archives.gov/publications/prologue/2009/winter/wra.html.

Solomon, Molly. "Once Lost, Internment Camp in Hawaii Now a National Monument." NPR Code Switch. Heard on Morning Edition, March 16, 2015. npr.org/sections/codeswitch /2015/03/16/393284680/in-hawaii-a-wwii-internment-camp -named-national-monument.

Stratton, Donald. *All the Gallant Men: The First Memoir by a USS* Arizona *Survivor.* New York: William Morrow, 2016.

Trumbull, Robert. "Pearl Harbor: One Day of Infamy, Two Years of Hard Work." Opinion. *New York Times.* December 7, 2006. Available online at nytimes.com/2006/12/07/opinion/07trumbull.html.

Twomey, Steve. *Countdown to Pearl Harbor: The Twelve Days to the Attack*. New York: Simon & Schuster, 2016.

Viotti, Vicki. "Partner Waited Lifetime for Last Dance." *Honolulu Advertiser*. December 4, 2001. the.honoluluadvertiser.com /article/2001/Dec/04/ln/ln04a.html.

Willamette University, Hatfield Library News. "1941 Pearl Harbor Willamette Football Team." December 17, 2015. library.willamette .edu/wordpress/blog/2015/12/17/1941-pearl-harbor-willamette -football-team.

# IMAGE CREDITS

George R. Caron/US Army (p. 154); John Collier/Library of Congress (p. 116); German Federal Archives/Bild 183-J30142 (p. 146); German Federal Archives/Bild 183-S55480 (p. 4); German Federal Archives/Bild 183-Z0309-310 (p. 148); Hawaii State Archives (p. 139); Lt. Stephen E. Korpanty/Naval Historical Center (p. 155); Staff Sergeant Louis R. Lowery/United States Marine Corps (p. 151); Kate Messner (pp. 44, 53, 179); Ministry of Information Second World War Press Agency Print Collection (p. 149); National Park Service (pp. 29, 62, 129); patchii/Shutterstock.com (p. 171); Sean Pavone/Shutterstock.com (p. 168); Pool/Kyodo News Stills via Getty Images (p. 172); Pung/Shutterstock.com (p. 162); Joe Rosenthal/National Archives and Records Administration (p. 150); Chief Photographer's Mate Robert F. Sargent/US Coast Guard (p. 147); Maurice Savage/Alamy Stock Photo (p. 170); Unknown photographer/US Navy (p. 73); US Army (pp. 133, 141); US Army Signal Corps (p. 93); US National Archives (pp. 79, 91, 97 106, 134, 157); US Post Office, Bureau of Engraving and Printing (p. 152).

# INDEX

# SMASH MORE STORIES!

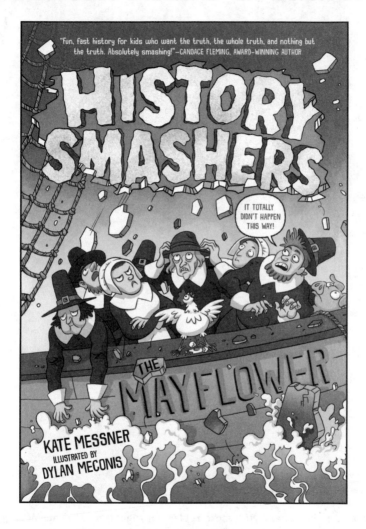

Turn the page for a peek at the first book
in the History Smashers series!

You've probably heard about the *Mayflower*. Chances are, someone told you about the Pilgrims, who came to America because they wanted religious freedom. You probably learned how they crossed the wild Atlantic, how they landed at Plymouth Rock in Massachusetts, how the Wampanoag people taught them to grow corn, and how they all celebrated by sitting down together for a feast—the very first Thanksgiving. But only parts of that story are true.

There's a lot more to the history of the *Mayflower*, the Pilgrims, and the Wampanoag. So let's take a look at the historical documents, smash some of those old myths, and uncover the *real* story.

# ONE
# WHO WERE THE PILGRIMS, ANYWAY?

I f April showers bring May flowers, what do May flowers bring?

The answer to the riddle, of course, is Pilgrims. The joke works because almost everyone knows a little about the Pilgrims. We've heard how they left England

and came to America in search of religious freedom. But that's not even close to the whole story. For starters, the Pilgrims didn't go to America when they left England. Not at first, anyway.

The real-deal story of the *Mayflower* begins way back in the 1530s, when King Henry VIII made some big changes to religion in England. King Henry wanted a son who could grow up to be the king of England, too. He and his first wife only had a daughter, though. Henry decided the solution was to get divorced and marry someone else, with whom he might have a son.

But the Roman Catholic Church was the official church in England then, and it did not allow divorce. King Henry went all the way to the pope, the leader of the whole Catholic Church, to argue that he should be able to leave his wife and marry a new one. When the pope said no, Henry decided to break away from the Catholic Church and start his own. From then on, the Church of England would be the official church of the land.

King Henry wasn't the only one who had issues with the Roman Catholic Church at that time. Many complained that Catholic leaders had too much power and wealth. But not everyone liked King Henry's new church, either. Some thought it was too similar to the Catholic Church. One group, called the Puritans, wanted the new church to be "purified" of all the old practices. Other people didn't think that was enough. They were called Separatists because they wanted to separate from the Church of England completely and have their own religion. The Separatists thought that true Christian believers should come together in their own small churches. They wanted those churches to be independent so members could study the Bible and make decisions on their own.

William Brewster, who was the postmaster of a village called Scrooby, decided to start a church in his own house. It was a risky idea. Back then, people who didn't follow the Church of England could be thrown in jail. In his book *Of Plymouth Plantation*, Pilgrim William Bradford wrote that Brewster's Separatists were "hunted and persecuted on every side."

Government officials were watching the Separatists' houses day and night. Some of them did get thrown in jail. You can probably understand why leaving England was starting to seem like a good idea.

So that's when the Separatists set sail for America, right?

Wrong. They went to Holland.

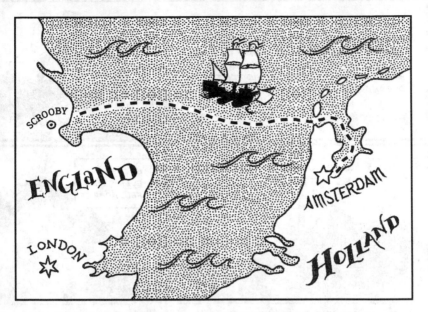

Holland, which today we call the Netherlands, was known for religious freedom. Brewster learned that a small group of Separatists had recently escaped to the city of Amsterdam, where they could practice their religion in peace. That seemed like a good idea, so Brewster made plans to take his group there, too. His followers were nervous, though. They didn't speak Dutch. They weren't sure how they'd earn money to support their families. Bradford later wrote that to many of the Separatists, taking off for Holland seemed like "an adventure almost desperate" and "a misery worse than death." But after much discussion, they decided to go anyway.

**1607:** BREWSTER ARRANGED FOR A SHIP TO SNEAK HIS CONGREGATION AWAY TO AMSTERDAM. IT WAS EXPENSIVE, AND THEY HAD TO WAIT A LONG TIME, BUT HE DIDN'T SEE ANY OTHER OPTION.

FINALLY THE DAY ARRIVED.

IT WAS TIME FOR THE SEPARATISTS TO LEAVE ENGLAND ONCE AND FOR ALL!

BUT THEN EVERYTHING FELL APART.

THE SHIP'S CAPTAIN HAD RATTED THEM OUT!

THE SHIP'S CREW RANSACKED ALL THE PASSENGERS' BELONGINGS,

LOOKING FOR MONEY.

THEY TURNED THE SEPARATISTS OVER TO THE AUTHORITIES.

INSTEAD OF ESCAPING TO HOLLAND,

THEY ENDED UP SPENDING A MONTH IN AN ENGLISH PRISON.

# SMASH MORE STORIES!

Turn the page for a peek at the second book
in the History Smashers series!

You've probably heard stories about how American women won the right to vote. Chances are, you learned about Susan B. Anthony, who fought for that right along with some of her friends.

It's true that for a long time in America, only men could vote. That went on for more than a hundred years, until women got so angry that they did something about it. Maybe this is where you've imagined Susan B. Anthony and her pals coming into the story— a group of women in fancy hats, drinking tea, writing letters, and talking about equality. But that's just a tiny part of what happened.

The true story about women's right to vote is a lot longer and more complicated than that. And Susan B. Anthony was just a part of that bigger picture—a story of women who worked together but also fought with one another. They argued over everything from who should get to vote to how they should go about making change.

Sometimes those women had one another's backs, and sometimes they didn't. Some of the same white women who talked and wrote about justice and equality fought hard to keep women of color living separate and unequal lives. Sometimes the women who fought for voting rights were heroes—and sometimes not so much. Some of them worked hard to hide the contributions of other heroes because of the color of their skin. In the end, the story of women's fight for the right to vote is a much messier one than history books like to share. Let's smash that old story! Here's the real deal. . . .

# ONE
# WHO IS A CITIZEN?

Today it's hard to imagine how anyone could argue that some Americans should get to vote while others shouldn't. To understand the fight for voting rights, you have to understand that for the European men who colonized America, inequality was a tradition. Most of those early colonists came from England, where married women weren't even allowed to own property. Everything those women owned before they got married suddenly belonged to their husbands after the wedding.

In England, you had to be a man who owned property in order to vote. The colonists brought that system with them when they settled on the other side of the ocean. The men who wrote America's founding documents, the Declaration of Independence and the Constitution, held on to those old ideas when they set up the new nation's government. The only real discussion of women's rights at that time came from their wives.

As America was getting ready to declare its independence from Great Britain in 1776, Abigail Adams raised the issue in a letter to her husband, future-president John Adams.

*In the new code of laws which I suppose it will be necessary for you to make, I desire you would remember the ladies and be more generous and favorable to them than your ancestors.*

It's probably no surprise to you that John ignored Abigail's advice. Eleven years later, he and the other men in charge of the new nation sat down to write the US Constitution, the document that would outline how the government would work. They spent weeks debating what should be included, but they never even talked about the possibility of women voting. For the men in that room, that just wasn't how things worked.

Before the Revolutionary War, individual colonies had all kinds of different laws about who could vote and who couldn't. Sometimes it was based on race. In much of the South, where many Black people were enslaved, even free Black men weren't allowed to vote. You had to be male *and* white. Native American men were allowed to vote in some colonies but not others. And in some places, voting rights depended on religion.

When the colonies broke away from England, the new states made their own rules about who could vote.

Some decided to stick with tradition, giving the vote to men who owned a certain amount of property. Other states changed things up a little. In New Jersey, men could vote if they had *either* fifty pounds' worth of property or money. Vermont decided to let all men vote, whether they owned anything or not.

When it was time to figure out voting rights on the national level, the men who wrote the Constitution talked about including a property rule. Some lawmakers loved that idea. They were mostly from the South, where men who owned lots of property wanted to keep power for themselves. But others argued that men who didn't own property were already voting in some states. If the Constitution included a property requirement, they'd lose a right they already had. That didn't seem fair at all.

As the men talked, two very different ideas about voting emerged. Some said voting was **a privilege you should have to earn** . . . somehow. (Usually by having enough money to own property.) Others argued that voting was **a natural right** that should be given to all people, and that it couldn't—or shouldn't—be taken away by anyone.

The committee argued about this question for more than a week during the hot, sticky summer of 1787. Finally the men reached an agreement. They decided . . . not to make a decision. They left the issue of who gets to vote out of the Constitution entirely. The original document never mentions gender or property requirements. It only explains that under the new government, "people" would choose their representatives.

Not people who own property.

Not men.

Just people.

At first you might think that sounds great. There are no restrictions on voting in the Constitution! Everybody gets to vote! Right?